D0966386

POETS FOR LIFE

POETS FOR
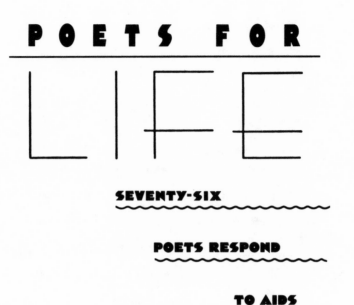

SEVENTY-SIX

POETS RESPOND

TO AIDS

Edited with an Introduction by Michael Klein
Essays by the Rt. Rev. Paul Moore, Jr.,
Joseph Papp, and Carol Muske

Crown Publishers, Inc.
New York

A detailed list of acknowledgments begins on p. 241.

Compilation and introduction copyright © 1989 by Michael Klein

Preface copyright © 1989 by the Rt. Rev. Paul Moore, Jr.

Foreword copyright © 1989 by Joseph Papp

"Rewriting the Elegy" copyright © 1989 by Carol Muske

Published by Crown Publishers, Inc., 225 Park Avenue South,
New York, New York 10003

CROWN is a trademark of Crown Publishers, Inc.

Manufactured in the United States of America

Library of Congress Cataloging-in-Publication Data

Poets for life.
1. AIDS (Disease)—Poetry.   2. AIDS (Disease)—
Patients—Poetry.   3. American poetry—20th century.
I. Klein, Michael.
PS595.A36P64   1989   811'.54'080356   88-35219
ISBN 0-517-52742-7

Book design by Linda Kocur

1   3   5   7   9   10   8   6   4   2

First Edition

Contents

TDC

Preface

The Rt. Rev. Paul Moore, Jr.,
Bishop of New York

Only poetry can express the complex depths, the whirlpools of despair, the agony of feeling betrayed, the passion, the nostalgia for youth, the holocaust of dying, the mysterious quality of gay and lesbian love. Only a poet can convey the tragic triple cross of color, addiction, and AIDS, the holy innocence of brown babies, black babies, white babies sentenced to death before their birth.

Most informed Americans have come to understand those medical facts about AIDS that have been established, how the disease is communicated, the terror of projected statistics. But the resonance of the spirits of those affected upon our culture and the first glimpses of its power are just beginning to surface. In the same way that the music and poetry of Negro spirituals enshrine forever the peculiar quality of black suffering and interpenetrates the culture of our land with the tragedy, the absurdity and the obscenity of that long agony, so do these poems begin to communicate the AIDS experience.

I have felt moments of grandeur and glory when names were spoken, one by one, in the dark and silent nave of the Cathedral of St. John the Divine. I have felt the love of God flow through my hands into the failing body of a friend and back to me as a blessing to us both. I have heard a Sister speak to me of the presence of the Kingdom of Love amongst the patients, families, care givers, and chaplains in the AIDS ward of St. Luke's Hospital. And I have sensed the strange shores of an alien land as I embraced the thin, disappearing body of a person with AIDS in peace and love.

Therefore, I am grateful that these poems have been gathered together so that we may use them as a Baedeker of the spirit for the dark travels that lie ahead.

Read them, return to them, meditate upon them so that you may be strengthened, guided, and inspired by the pain and beauty they contain.

F o r e w o r d

J o s e p h   P a p p

While reading a manuscript copy of the AIDS poems compiled by Michael Klein, my thoughts drifted back to 1939...bleak times; the worst of times. I am working in a laundry after school on 15th Street in Manhattan. I pass a newsstand and my heart stops; the headline: MADRID FALLS. Not wanting to spend the money, I sneak a glance at the front page. Half the story is concealed by an iron weight, carefully placed by the vendor to encourage customer curiosity and a sale. I make out a few of the lines: "Generalissimo Francisco Franco enters...Hitler jubilant as he...Democracies silent."

I head back home for Brooklyn. My thoughts are gloomy and fearful. This is without a doubt, I think, the worst time in my life. At least I thought it was—at 17.

Years later, I am browsing through books at an old shop on Fourth Avenue. I come across a splendid and unusual set of Shakespeare's plays—practically new. Each of the plays is individually bound in a cheerful beige and golden cover. The elegant pages are of a rough stock with Elizabethan-styled type, large and invitingly readable, and drawings by distinguished artists of the 1930s.

I am overjoyed to have stumbled upon this treasure and can hardly wait to open and peruse each and every lovely volume. It is when I turn a page in *The Tempest* that an old yellowed newspaper clipping falls out. It is a *New York Times* book review heralding the publication and, to my amazement, dated 1939.

I am struck by the thought that had I been a *Times* reader instead of a *Daily News/Daily Mirror* reader in those terrible days, I might have read that review in 1939, and how my flagging spirits would have soared at the great news—"Shakespeare has come to town! Away gloom and doom! Poetry reigns and its hopeful light shines through the darkness forcing the rats of the world to cover their eyes and scurry for cover." For they find this light unbearable.

"Poetry and its hopeful light"—I am back to the manuscript copy of the AIDS poems. The year 1939 becomes 1989 and I realize I am performing some kind of act of digression, even evasion. For some strange and mysterious reason I find myself unable or unwilling to fulfill my promise to Crown Publishers for some few words of introduction to their forthcoming book, *Poets for Life: 76 Poets Respond to AIDS,* the manuscript that I hold in my hands. I waste no more time, pick up my pad and pencil, and quickly begin to write. The words come easily. I believe them deeply... the importance of poetry in times of crisis and how, like the publication of the Shakespeare canon in the midst of a world on the brink of war, poetry becomes a vote for humanity, a proclamation for life.

The lead worn down, my pencil needs sharpening. My mind is racing with the whir of the electric sharpener. I write of the healing power of poetry. I raise the question: "Can poetry, mere words joined together, be an effective weapon against AIDS?" I answer yes. In the spirit of 1939, I find myself writing "Like enemy propaganda in war, words play a vital role in winning that war." I continue with grim determination: "All of us, people with AIDS and people without, are in this together." I feel an ache around my heart. My fingers are growing numb. "How we think, how we verbalize the issues, our *state of mind* (I underline that phrase) must be strong and healthy to carry on the fight."

This last line bothers me. It sounds rhetorical, not personal. It's too coldly political. Something nourishing is called for. "The poems fill me with sadness, with anger, with love—a prescription to ward off the enemy, despair."

The ache in my heart is spreading to my chest and moves into my throat. I need to end, finish the assignment. "Poetry has always been the source for the most intimate and most tender expressions of human creativity. This is a time for poetry, a time that compels us to reach deep down . . ." I stop writing. I cannot continue. The ache is overwhelming and my throat is terribly tight. The concluding sentence is poised in my head, but I cannot write it.

The pen rests on the pad I am using. I look at the half-written page and I am surprised to find it smudged. It is wet. I am crying.

I pick up my fallen pencil. Begin to write. My God! I am writing a poem!

> DAYS GO SWIFTLY
> THE SUN RISES
> SOMETIMES WITH SPARKLING BRILLIANCE
> THE SUN OF MY CHILDHOOD
> FILLING ME WITH SUCH HAPPINESS
> ONLY POSSIBLE IN THE YOUNG
> (THAT HAS NOT YET LEARNED OF DEATH),
> AND THE PROMISE OF SPRING
> ENTERS MY CONSCIOUSNESS
> AND I AM ALIVE WITH HOPE AND EXPECTATION.
> MY THOUGHTS ARE OF SCHOOL DAYS,
> OF BROTHERS AND SISTERS,
> PARENTS AND TEACHERS,
> FRIENDS. . . .
> AT THE WORD
> MY EYES BEGIN TO DIM
> MY HEART ACHES OF AN ABSENCE
> AND A GREAT LONGING SWELLS UP WITHIN ME.
> LIKE THE CRY OF A WILD BIRD
> I HEAR THE NAME . . . WILFORD, WILFORD . . .

Ah, dear friend whose radiant humanity touched all who had the good fortune of knowing you, how I miss the wonder of you. My fallen comrade. Dear, dear friend.

Rewriting the Elegy

Carol Muske

Perhaps the single positive contribution of AIDS to our culture is a politics of death. That is to say, AIDS (like the Right to Die movement) has made dying itself—in bed, away from the battle-field—a political act. Death remains as personal as ever, but now everyone must bear witness to the rapid, brutal, sweeping dis-appearances of human beings. Everyone must hear (because we have a government that refuses to listen) what the dying have to say about how they will die, where they will die, what their right to treatment encompasses, how they wish the living to care for them, how they wish to be let go. To paraphrase Auden, we must pay attention, or die.

I feel the newness of this politics throughout this collection of poems. The dying have voices, finally: angry, intuitive, dreamy, fearful, eloquent, funny. Listening to them changes the way we write about death. Perhaps, as editor Michael Denneny has sug-gested, we will see in the growing body of AIDS literature, in-cluding this anthology, a literary "renaissance." The community of the dead and the dying and those who sit by the beds in homes and hospices and transient hotels, writing, will change forever how we imagine death. It seems to me that we have left behind us the tradition of "let the dead bury their dead." *These* dead will not lie quiet in their graves.

> At the wake, the tension broke
> when someone guessed
>
> the casket was closed because
> "he was in there in a big wig
> and heels," and someone said,

"You know he was always late,
he probably wasn't there yet—
he's still fixing his makeup."

Mark Doty, "Tiara"

Certainly death has been our most political enemy, a master
strategist when blocked and, with the advent of AIDS, reverting
to archetype: the unconquerable primitive specter, leaping han-
dily over the immunological beachheads of the twentieth century, trailing its centuries-long cape of fevers, cancers, bacilli.

Now death has advanced its politics to all-out war, or plague,
undermining the body's defenses, exploding the autoimmune
system, replacing it with a primary, staggering medical irony (a
disease which destroys the destroyers of disease) as well as ironies philosophical and literary. We make love and death at the
same time. It is literally possible to die of love.

the elegies are writing themselves
on desire's sheets, passion and suffering
are fusing their etymological roots
into a single trunk. *Yet why should they not embrace,
these beautiful two?* They are, after all, part
of the oldest story in the world—before God,
before microbes, before the sea had licked
the earth and the air clean with its long tongue.

Michael Blumenthal, "No More Kissing—
AIDS Everywhere"

Or as Heather McHugh puts it: "... Nobody knows/how your
disease is spread; it came/from love, or some/such place."

As passion and suffering fuse, we think of Keats, half in love
with easeful death—but the angle is sharper, crueler.

My thoughts are crowded with death
and it draws so oddly on the sexual
that I am confused to be attracted
by, in effect, my own annihilation.

Thom Gunn, "In Time of Plague"

7

Facing death has given these poems a common urgency, but without a collective viewpoint. Poets with vastly different sensibilities and styles have responded with similar rhetorical intent —to mobilize the reader to pity, to anger or compassion. Mallarmé said that everything in the world exists to end in a book. Writers are all too familiar with the daily implacability of this literary dictum, as their lives routinely become the substance of their art. In writing about AIDS, the mind reels: Can all this death be a like substance? The mind *resists:* Is it possible that this monolith, this unspeakable *wall* of grief, will be scribbled on too? With gravestone graffitti? Survivor ego?

But these poems are not the glib eulogies of survivors, millers of literary grist, they are the stunned words of the bloodied. They neither diminish *nor* sensationalize the horror. They eschew the falseness of the *natur morte;* they haven't the rigid, glossy beauties of the still life; they seem, in fact, to stagger under the burdensome cliché of the natural order, of death's sanctimonious inevitability. There is collective amazement that this is how death is entering our bodies—that the disease is *not* a technological invention, a sci-fi plot, a nightmare. What is conveyed, in poem after poem, is wonder that these words ever got written. There is an uncharacteristic (for contemporary poetry) lack of self-absorption; and thus, the poems seem oddly, attractively, unfinished, in the sense of a literary finish: Mallarmé's perfunctory poetic end to all existence.

Despite their varying tones, the poems in this anthology seem to hit the page at the same velocity. A fast slow-motion. We move in a terrible false parallel motion with those dying of AIDS, we struggle to keep up at the same time as we outdistance them.

> Terror has made us real enough
> to touch
> almost intimate . . .

Deborah Digges, "Faith-Falling"

People who have AIDS turn the mirror we hold to their lips around to our terrified faces. In an eerily transparent moment in a poem about his friend's blindness, Paul Monette leads Roger

down the sidewalk and asks him what fragment he still sees of
the world.

> you stop peer impish intent as a hawk
> and say *I see you* just like that . . .

> Paul Monette, "Your Sightless Days"

The startled fixity of that gaze is on every page of this book.
The dying see us. The faces looking out are not the legions of
Munch-like "death had undone so many" phantoms, but are real
as Roger, intent as hawks watching us, lovers, friends, parents,
children.

The elegy itself is changing. It has always been a competent
traditional vessel to hold grief and praise of the dead. Now it
seems to overflow, shatter, reform.

> Back from what he could neither
> Accept, as one opposed,
> Nor, as a life-long breather,
> Consentingly let go,
> The tube his mouth enclosed
> In an astonished O.

> Thom Gunn, "Still Life"

> You are not the target, you're the arrow
> and the dirty wind that hits
> your face on summer streets these
> too-long evenings means you're moving
> faster than you know, a shrill
> projectile through the neutral air
> above a world war . . .

> Tim Dlugos, "Retrovir"

The elegiac form, like a graveside path, has been worn smooth
in places by the years, but the language of these poems is direct
and unsparing in detail; it refuses literary phrasing or the phrasing of the eulogy. Part of what fuels the unconventional response
is the incongruousness of the dying themselves. The young and

strong are disappearing, people at the height of their careers and talents. Children are dying. It is a monumental task to find words for any elegy. To describe the loss of so many who should have lived into the next century strains all our notions of composition.

I knew Roger Horwitz, Paul Monette's friend. It is inconceivable to me that he is dead. Yet I stood at his funeral and witnessed his burial. It is also inconceivable to me that five-year-old Zachary Jacob Fried, who attended the same pre-school as my daughter, is dead. Zack died of AIDS, having received at birth an "infiltrated" transfusion from the Cedars Sinai blood bank.

Zack's name is on a quilt that travels the country like a post-dated letter from the dead.

> We are all made of
> our own people
> laying names on the ground
>
> Michael Klein,
> "Naming the Elements"

The AIDS quilt keeps Zack looking back at us—a small, pale, gifted child who drew beautiful pictures for his friends. Zack even offered a kind of elegy for himself, when he wondered aloud to his mother during the height of his suffering what it would be like to be a "let go balloon."

I would like to add Zack's elegy to this collection. It is tempting to think of the book itself as a kind of "let go balloon," rising away from suffering. But it isn't. Certainly, as Deborah Digges says in her poem "Faith-Falling," "on earth you can say goodbye." This anthology of poems must belong to this time on earth. It is both testimony and triumph—what elegy can be when we find the right words to match our grief.

Introduction

Michael Klein

One cool October morning in 1987, as the harsh, amber light gave Washington, D.C., its eerie, documentary look, the Names Project of San Francisco unfolded on the Capitol Mall a quilt commemorating Americans dead from AIDS. Faced with an endless succession of names and mementoes of photographs, sheet music, letters, teddy bears, clothing and fabrics ranging from satin to canvas, I walked through those panels and felt about the quilt what one viewer named Woody Mosely felt: "... so much like being in a cemetery. But it's different. It also feels alive."

I found myself coming back to the quilt during most of the day, and by the time the sky slowly began losing its chilly light I began to imagine how the quilt might look from an aerial perspective—like a map of a new country. While friends and strangers left the site, I watched the Names Project volunteers fold up the enormous memorial with the same solemnity one would fold a flag. Many of them were crying. As night moved across the slowly uncovered grass of the Mall, I found a broader solace in the quilt. To the ones in America who tried to ignore AIDS or who held contempt for people with AIDS, this American folk-art project would be a stunning reminder that those who are dead, and those who still suffer, are loved.

Like many of those who have walked among the quilt, I have marched and shouted against AIDS. I have held sick men in my arms, lost them and grieved; I have feared for my own life and the lives of people I love. For thousands of men and women, creating a panel for the quilt and sending it to a storefront in San Francisco was *their* way of enlisting in the crusade. After that day in Washington, D.C., I saw I could take part in both memorial and crusade as they had. I would do it through poetry.

That night I wrote a poem called "Naming the Elements," in which I compared the Vietnam Veterans Memorial with the Names Project and how they both respond in hard, visual ways to two American wars I will always remember with utter devastation—wars that should never have been allowed to take place. It occurred to me that I had started work on a quilt forming in my mind: by writing my own stanza for what would eventually become a much larger poem.

In December 1987, I read two poems in *Poetry* that were clearly about AIDS. Robert Cording's "Elegy to John, My Student Dead of AIDS" and David Bergman's "In the Waiting Room" rekindled a fire that had been started two months before when I sat in a living room overlooking the tranquil Adams-Morgan section of Washington, D.C, and wrote part of my contribution. Poets were responding to AIDS. *This* quilt would be a book.

I decided that an anthology of poems with AIDS as its subject would bring the poetry community together and perhaps create an opportunity to raise money for a cause related to fighting AIDS. I wrote to Mr. Cording and Mr. Bergman asking if they'd contribute their work. *Poets for Life* soon had two more stanzas. I knew that if the book was going to be as varied as it had to be, then I was going to have to solicit poems from people who may not have written on the subject before. Robert Cording, David Bergman, Thom Gunn, Felice Picano, Paul Monette, Heather McHugh, and Mark Doty all had written on AIDS already, but I suspected that many other poets were meditating long and hard about today's great crisis of love and death.

I contacted close to 300 poets about the idea of making a book. My only qualification for judging good from bad poetry is that I have read a lot of both. Hayden Carruth, Edward Field, David Groff, and J. D. McClatchy were helpful in steering me toward poems I might have missed otherwise.

What impressed me most about the poems I chose was how absolutely nonsensational they were. These were poems whose feelings seemed to be discovered *as* they were being written— not ramblings that supported preconceived ideas about AIDS. I was fortunate as well to be able to include work here by people with AIDS and people who have tested seropositive for HIV, the virus that most believe causes AIDS.

In the early stages of collecting material, I seemed to find elegies falling from the trees. And although this was not intended solely as a book of elegies (I'd point to *Love Alone: 18 Elegies for Rog* by Paul Monette, for that), a spirit of recollection permeates this anthology as I felt it permeating that day in Washington.

The critic David Kalstone (who died of AIDS-related causes) has been remembered by several writers. He was a friend of both Adrienne Rich (see her poem "In Memoriam") and James Merrill, who, in "Farewell Performance," recalls Kalstone as a lover of ballet—to which Merrill accompanied him often:

> Art. It cures affliction. As lights go down and
> Maestro lifts his wand, the unfailing sea change
> starts within us. Limber alembics once more
> make of the common
>
> lot a pure, brief gold. At the end our bravos
> call them back, sweat-soldered and leotarded,
> back, again back—anything not to face the
> fact that it's over.

I did not want this to be a book that looked only at the past or at death. I wanted it to be a book that would, in an odd way, celebrate a mystery. AIDS does more than cause us to grieve; it is both a reality and a metaphor for the most elemental human challenges. Poetry is able to sustain more than only grief and I wanted poems that arose out of as many different kinds of experience as possible, just as the quilt had been sewn together from as many different kinds of material. Besides elegies, you'll find represented here narratives about plague, children and family, time spent in waiting rooms, time spent in hospitals, time spent in staying alive.

Paul Monette's work is about staying alive. Through lack of formal punctuation in some poems, and utilization of long fluid lines, he demonstrates a blazing virtuosity with language. His poems are as urgent as the headlines that inspire them. His passion for life, coupled with his rage against our country's handling of AIDS, have made him an outstanding artist and spokesman for those who must confront AIDS every day. He is one of the few writers here who openly address Washington, corporations, and politicians:

> . . . oh Buckley the thing is I agree
> about Soviet wheat the Shah the Joint Chiefs
> can have all the toilet seats they like but
> somehow your pantaloons are in a froth
> to cheerlead the dying of my pink people
> covered with a condom head to toe St. Paul
> of the boneyard guillotining dicks . . .

> Paul Monette, "Buckley"

The daily struggle in living with AIDS and in loving someone with AIDS is represented in poems like David Trinidad's "Driving Back From New Haven," which speaks so simply for so many:

> Tim looks at his watch, reaches into his
> pocket, takes out a small plastic container
> and swallows an AZT pill with a sip of Sprite.
> 'Poison,' he mutters under his breath . . .

In "Maybe the Jay," Robin Behn personalizes anger and fear over the very fact of viral infection until it haunts us:

> . . . My cousin has tested
> positive, it seems. Positive. As if
>
> the virus could cheer you up, as in
> "think positive," or the "I'm positive, dear!"
>
> that sends the two-lovers-and-then-some,
> kissing, back to bed.
>
> It's as if her anorectic frame that always looked
> like a negative has suddenly gathered flesh, and now
>
> she's walking out, backlit, into 3-D
> to borrow our futures. Oh, my cousin
>
> is positive, positive:
> more than the zero she believed herself to be;
>
> more than the plus of the cross hairs
> through which, in terrible retrospect,

we see her crooked arm, the shared
needle of happiness; more

than the charge of glass rubbed with silk
(her glass thighs, the silk

hood hiding the boy's face from us
so we won't blame him, later).

I think of anger as the state of fear waking up. Robert Louthan's
"Syndrome" is another haunting poem of rage at its most alive:

When we're done with this embrace,
which is final and encumbered with the gun
I've brought to bed because our loving was diseased
and you're dazzled now daily by pain . . .

And finally, there are people with AIDS who plan very much
to keep on living—in spite of the lack of consistent government
funding for research or treatment, in spite of having to shout
with passion and rage into an atrocity of silence:

They keep taking away your future
like your driver's license.
They don't want you back on the road.
Statistics: live barbed wire
around your genitals.
And you, who no longer separate
the red heart
from the breaking one,
you, whose living they can't explain
you grow unmistakably
solidly round
like Buddha.

Eve Ensler, "For Richard"

The Quilt: Stories From the NAMES Project tells of how many
people who made panels found the experience something they
didn't expect—sometimes the panel didn't turn out as they had
envisioned. In letters accompanying the submissions to *Poets for
Life,* many writers said the same thing about their contributions:
Their poems turned into different things. Michael Cadnum, for
instance, found writing about AIDS difficult—but after he fin-

ished "Desert" he felt that he had been guided through his own imagined inability to deal with it. Perhaps Joseph Hansen put it best about writing and AIDS when he referred to his novel *Early Graves:*

> ... reading of how doctors, nurses, police and fire personnel, school teachers, clergymen were dealing with AIDS, or recoiling as some did in fear and loathing; of how panicky politicians were making life worse for the already dying; of how men and women in and out of power talked and talked while the victims of vicious pneumonia, skin cancer, parasite of gut and eye and brain, wasted away—reading this stuff day after day at last began to show me what I must write and how I must write it. There was no way around it for me.

Marvin Bell, Kevin Clarke, Jean Valentine, and Robert Creeley, among others, had never written about AIDS before they were approached for this anthology. I believe poets have been responding to AIDS with the sense that they are providing a kind of historical text to this epidemic. As we have had actors, dancers, musicians, and painters fight against AIDS, we can now add the words of the writers collected here who have donated their work. A percentage in sales of this book will go to the PEN Emergency Fund for Writers and Editors with AIDS.

As it has diminished community after community, AIDS has also strangely united us. As it has summoned still more fear and uncertainty in the way we live, AIDS has revealed more courage and understanding about how we affect each other. The issues AIDS insists we confront are the most timeless and immediate of all: the battle between love and death. None of us is exempt from that battle. No one is immune. AIDS has forced us into a firmer embrace of our own lives, which we must fight for day after day. It has given us an awareness into how to fight for life with an entirely new sense of immediacy.

Although the age hasn't dawned in which a poem can actually kill a virus and save a life, I hope the poems you are holding will, as Wallace Stevens said about all poems, help you to live your life. I hope the book does what all well-made quilts are meant to do—last awhile, keep you warm.

POETS FOR
LIFE

The Gifts

for Lea Baechler

Most of my friends and all of my past
lovers wait for news of one kind or another. Waking
in separate rooms, our breath warms laceworks
of frost. One died four days before Hallowe'en,
nearly weightless. I think of metaphors

for marking time: windows, the torn pockets
of winter coats and what falls through, lost
for good. Tomorrow, you leave
for the merciful country, that place where no one
dies (or so I imagine). I don't know

who we meant to be in different lives
though, once, the ground beneath planes seemed
a window we'd learn to fall through, given
the chance. Now, we move through these rooms
slowly, sit by windows and address

the reverberating light outside,
wishing prayer were more than a collection
of beautiful words: *I am poured out
like water* . . . Once, in a graveyard north
of Pittsburgh, we stood before

a cinder block chapel with smoke-
glass doors and Jesus fixed to the outside wall;
Mary looked up from his terrible feet
to his stainless steel ribs, thin as the blades
of pocket knives. It wasn't pity written

on her face. I want to tell you
that I'm dying, I don't know who we'll be
when you return, or if January will hold together
the bones of need. Last winter, you carried me
north on Seventh Avenue,

my arms around your shoulders and my legs
around your waist, the two of us drunk enough
to wake in a movie house where the gorgeous
fucked on screen and the desperate between reels.
And none can keep alive his own

soul . . . Out of grief comes rage,
as, years ago, I watched the power lines
around my father's house burn, flames
shot through with blue electric sustenance.
I stood on the lawn and waited for the danger

to pass. The danger never once
came close enough, until now. This morning,
after waking enough for the world,
I walked the markets of Hell's Kitchen,
gathering our dinner. Home again

and short of breath, I climb the stairs,
reach for the door as though for grace.
The stock boils now, a landscape of fervent air.
The sliced flesh of vegetables goes into the pot
and we wait. Once more, the bare December

trees beneath this window bend,
their living branches greet one another
and bend. Tonight, we'll bow our heads
over steaming bowls of late abundance,
whisper our separate graces for the living, the dead—

blessed, the gifts we receive.

■

A Diagnosis

E.M.H., 1944–1988

Friend, yes, the winter following
a diagnosis seems the longest winter
   of them all. The bones recall how, thick
with cold, the late December air
   chilled those rooms we'd gather to undo:
      the usual photographs,
         the clothes, the letters of the dead . . .

      "What is the light like there?"
one letter begins. "A bed by a window
   facing the gardened center of the block—
the late afternoon sun must be brilliant!
   The light here? A fog obscures the odd parabolas
      of light across the East River: the signature,
         Pepsi-Cola, in letters larger than life;

      fog, or a trick of the eye."
How this weather impersonates our loss,
   the body used then useless, battered ephemera.
Waste, wasting, wasted . . . the rooms and the terrible
   flesh undone. Our homes abandon us,
      like skin. Mornings, we scrutinize limbs
         for the rude stigmata of our kind,

      as map-makers their memories
for islands. "Lastly, to record our travels,
   as by our travels the world
remembers us." From a neighbor's window
   a greenish light's thrown off, a lamp
      glancing the leaves of house plants;
         its radiance waters into black,

the blackness poured out like water.
Midtown, the towers rise, a Jacob's ladder.
I will not let thee go, except thou bless me.
Friend, our unanswerable letters forbid grief,
their language these constantly-from-a-distance
goodbyes, the valedictions of a compass
fixed and tracing at once.

■

Identifying Things

Is diabetes catching, he asks,
middle-school braggadocio edged
this time with something else, I can't
quite put my finger on it,
until he tells about the needle,
that kid Jamie, jabbing a needle he had picked up
on the street, punctured far into the flesh
of my son's palm.

Trouble boils a greasy steam into the air.
Whose needle, what kind, whose veins
had it entered? My son, my son, only eleven
years old and the doctor over the phone doesn't help,
his nurse says you bet, plenty to worry about,
and it's not just AIDS we'd want to run tests for,
there's hepatitis, three strains now—find the needle,
bring in the needle, make sure those boys
find that needle.

                Under the oaks
a new kind of bird flocks at the feeder,
I have no idea what they are, they swarm
and dart around the perches, on the ground,
they are everywhere, and outside their shrill
wheezing chokes out the drone of trucks on the interstate.

So he will teach us death, perhaps.
We will allow him the perfect death.
We will all work on dying

together, we will give him that, and maybe
it won't even happen, maybe the needle
belonged to Jamie, he's a diabetic,
maybe it was just one of his own insulin needles,
probably there is nothing in the world
to worry about, chances are slim, we mustn't
upset our boy, mustn't blow this out
of proportion.

           I can't identify
the birds. They are too streaked
for goldfinches, they could be
warblers, winter plumage, but their beaks
are a little thicker, I'm just not sure
and none of these walls
line up straight.

When the boys find the needle and take it
to the principal and you stop by school
our kid is most upset because his father
is actually seen by his friends, only nerds have
parents who enter this territory,
he will never live it down, his own father
picking him up in front of his friends,
driving him to the doctor's. Just a little needle,
the kind for pricking a finger for small
blood samples, adults always overreact.
The doctor and the nurses laugh out loud,
at home the walls rise crisp
to the ceiling where the light dances.

          And the new birds
are pine siskins, yes, they are,
just a little yellow on the wings and tail,
it helps, it always helps when you know
what things are.

■

ROBIN BEHN

Maybe the Jay

Maybe the jay resting on the eve right now
is really all mirrors: just a fake blue

stolen from the sky-blue sky.
And the sky's just a blue mote

in Your enormous eye—You,
so big, so pleased with Yourself,

so distantly wondering how we
could subscribe to the theory that sex

makes birds dress up in blue.
How they project themselves into everything,

You think, and shrug, and a tidal wave ensues.
But what have You done different

if we are to believe
"In its own image, God, the parent, made . . ."

and what about this news
that flies in, airmail, in sync

with the jay? My cousin has tested
positive, it seems. Positive. As if

the virus could cheer you up, as in
"think positive," or the "I'm positive, dear!"

that sends the two-lovers-and-then-some,
kissing, back to bed.

It's as if her anorectic frame that always looked
like a negative has suddenly gathered flesh, and now

she's walking out, backlit, into 3-D
to borrow our futures. Oh, my cousin

is positive, positive:
more than the zero she believed herself to be;

more than the plus of the cross hairs
through which, in terrible retrospect,

we see her crooked arm, the shared
needle of happiness; more

than the charge of glass rubbed with silk
(her glass thighs, the silk

hood hiding the boy's face from us
so we won't blame him, later).

And if we've been deficient
in love up till now,

if we didn't orbit her,
a family of electrons, and follow

those clinical "positive suggestions"
we paid for by the hour,

we admit that, though wise,
we should have been wiser,

nobler, now,
we are not Noblest, but

You are, You are,
You are, You are,

so keep
her little plus-sign aloft on your radar

until we find the cure
or at least find one needle

sharp as love's *l*, filled with sufficient
belief to kill the symptoms.

■

The Plague

Then all the evidence we have of who is
missing in the general convolution
of what we call our "sky," talking prose,
or "heaven," hoping now for absolution,

is the white holes in a cloth hung to cover
the corpse of outer space, as dead to us
as the porchlight flickering after the foreign movers,
after a labored day, drive off with the bus.

A puppet stage, through whose quivering curtain
we once took note of certain bodily presences,
which metaphor could serve, when life seemed certain,
now falls around the dolls where innocence is.

Many are gone or going. We see the light
that comes from a cold star and know the outcome.
At last report there was more still to night
than stars, or yet to life than heaven and home.

■

DAVID BERGMAN

A Dream of Nightingales

In memory of Jerry Thompson

The Friday before your funeral I taught
Keats to my sophomore class. Little did they care
for the truth of beauty or the grace of truth,
but his being "half in love with easeful death"
penetrated through the smugness of their youth,
and I thought of you drawing me to the rear
window one early spring to hear in rapture
a bird hidden among the flowering pear.

You held your cat tight so that he could not scare
off such music as hadn't been heard all winter.
When you flew South to escape the arctic blast
and home again heard that dark-winged creature sing,
tell me, did he then reveal himself at last
as you believed he'd be—pure and beckoning?

■

In the Waiting Room

St. Gaudens would have known what would suit
this research institution: a tall,
stately figure of Science, proudly
undeterred, her plain draperies hung
in even rows to soften the cast
of her bronze body, one hand aloft
raising a hypodermic needle.

Before such images these six-month
check-ups would seem like a pilgrimage
in which unpardonable clerics
and unbathed wives had walked before me.
But in this vast, unadorned building
there's no distraction from my purpose
or the object for which I've journeyed.

With only the pages of *People*
and *Time* for amusement, who would not
feel afraid? For I am here as part
of a study on the life cycle
of the adult homosexual,
to see which of us will sicken next
in our group of twelve hundred odd

from this strange disease of yet unknown
beginnings that teaches the body
how to betray the life within it.
An endangered species, we are watched
to see how it makes its first appearance
and all the stages on which it acts
in our theatre of operations.

Sometimes two or three men are waiting
to be called—not by name—but number
to preserve our anonymity
(though who in the face of such cool
clinical detachment could retain
a sense of self). Yet at times one might
see a friend or distant acquaintance

head down or looking at the wall
(there are no windows here) marking where
the plaster has given way. I stop,
exchange a few meaningless phrases

and perhaps he'll have a joke to tell
or news of someone known in common
until the silence descends once more.

And once, early for my appointment,
I was left alone when voices shot
through swinging doors. A man in a white
laboratory coat and another
clad in jeans were speaking, and I knew
that the man in denim had become
the person I feared that I might be.

And I hated him for having brought
his death so near that I could touch it,
and the room seemed to fill with the dread
odor of his dying, and I sat amazed:
for with his neat beard and curly hair
and the whiteness of his freckled face,
he might be taken for my lover.

Now the two were arguing in that
complicitous tone of handymen
faced with a machine that will not work.
What about this? Or that? they question,
uncertain which, if any, repairs
to undertake, running their cold hands
along the ailing anatomy.

"I'll never live through *that*," the patient
laughs, as though it were another's case
he were discussing. I asked myself,
can this be true? Can people withdraw
so far from their existence that life
and death become academic games
left to pique their curiosity,

a trivial pursuit that will not
bore when played for hours at a time?
Or is there some catharsis unknown
to me, when what you fear will happen
happens and there's nothing more to fear,
and one reaches that calm meadow where
the sacred few are allowed to rest

beyond the walled, polluted city
that cast them out? They are gone away
now out of sight through another set
of fire doors, but their voices still
can be heard faintly like a new spring
or the hushed tones of lovers careful
not to wake the disapproving crowd.

A nurse approaches, clipboard in hand.
Have I brought my paraphernalia,
samples of semen and excrement
which the study cannot do without?
And the old terror revives in me
of what they will find: the truth, perhaps,
that I like everyone else will die.

Bring him back, bring him back, the one who
gave me this healing touch. I'm ready
to embrace him now if he can stop
the pain of losing what was never
mine to keep. Bring him back
so that he can teach me how to be
content when I take his place at last.

■

No More Kissing — AIDS
Everywhere

He says it to the young couple
passionately kissing on the street
and, when he does, the four of us just stand there,
laughing, on this cold wintry day in Cambridge,
nineteen hundred and eighty-eight,
as if there could be no such danger
to a kiss, as if the metaphors of love and dying
had not been literalized.

Pausing a block later, my cheeks kissed
by the cold, my lips cracking
in the January air, I think back
to what a man once told me, long before
risk had so clinical a name,
so precise a passage. *"You must remember,"*
he said, *"that every time you make love
you tamper with fate."*

Now, the early wisdoms grow clear:
the serpents slither into the yard,
the elegies are writing themselves
on desire's sheets, passion and suffering
are fusing their etymological roots
into a single trunk. *Yet why should they not embrace,
these beautiful two?* They are, after all, part
of the oldest story in the world—before God,
before microbes, before the sea had licked
the earth and the air clean with its long tongue.

They are, finally, that last metaphor
we have all been waiting for: standing
on a cold corner in this village of the intellect,
breathing their young lives into each other's lungs,
kissing their way towards heaven till they die.

■

PHILIP BOOTH

Marches

Sun just up on the century's earliest equinox;
patchy snow in the woods, ice not yet out,
woodcock migrating into the alder thickets.
Far from woodsheds with less than a dry cord left,

the young winter-out on their counter-migrations;
wading the surf, getting wasted, pretending
they cannot die, and will not, as long as
their bodies tan, and burn to feel each other's.

Far in the desert, out to arrest their government,
twelve hundred women and men, hands linked against
a chainlink fence, give themselves to arrest.
Handcuffed, shunted to barbed-wire camps, they delay

the test for twenty-four hours. In which new day
thousands of death-needles are passed, uncountable
lovers die shunned by their parents, hundreds of
children are born with systems in no way immune.

And millions of the rest of us, self-righteous
in the perfect democracy of back-country roads, freeways,
and interstates, pass each other at life-span speeds;
or close, in opposing lanes, at a hundred and thirty,

trusting implicitly in simple self-interest, missing
each other, time after time, only by fragments of seconds,
as we move our lives, or dyings, another round toward
what March may be like in maybe the year 2000.

■

Talking to Jim

So nothing is left of your agony.
Already your friends remember
your service, splendid occasion.
Your final lover talks only of

you, everyone's pleased he has
a new friend. Your sister's
defying your will, trying to
have you declared insane, adding

you were trying to go straight.
I remember when KS reached the
tip of your nose *I'll never be
ready for my close-up now,* you

said in the living room. No one
was reaching for the camera.

■

Mercy

Out in the harbor breaths of smoke
are rising from the water, sea-smoke
some call it or breath of souls,

the air so cold the great salt mass
shivers and, underlit, unfurls the ghosts
transfigured in its fathoms, some

having died there, most aslant
the packed earth to this lassitude,
this liquid recollection

of god's eternal mood. All afternoon
my friend counts from her window
the swaths like larkspur in a field of land

as if she could absorb their emanations
and sorting through them find the one
so recent to my grief, which keeps,

she knows, my eyes turned from the beach.
She doesn't say this, only, have you seen
the sea-smoke on the water, a voice absorbed

by eyes and eyes by those
so close to home, so ready to resume
the lunge of a desire, rested and clear of debris

they leave, like waking angels rising
on a hint of wind, visible or unseen, a print,
a wrinkle on the water.

■

Walk on the Water

Chafed ocean, a chadored moon
fluting the supple acres,
the silver spine of surf drawn from

a shore still resonant, each sounding
molecule discrete yet filled
with sameness so continuous

we might believe you too
though drawn from us instill
us who are left

with eucalyptus resin on our fingers,
after the flowers,
torn from styromoss,

have drowned the hollow grave its sound
of metal against bone, although
the earth was rained on, soft

the hands on the shovel as if one last time
your arm—peace
is that continuity,

you were trying to tell us,

faithful and loyal to the last
you were cast from, friend
in the vibrant elements,

song without skin to hold.

■

All day you stare at us
who may not touch
your weeping or your blood.
Heather McHugh

Kind, kind, milk in the mind
milk in the child, child in the blind
hormone of sleep, at night, supine

paralysand, flat as a star
soaked in the hopeful calcium all mammals
like a prayer paging god lie down

to weep out for our young, mild
soporific milk endure my cry
issuing ineluctable

and somewhat like a bird
in flight out of an oil spill, a black
bird that had just been white, a brother

from the cratered tit, aureoled, blue, perennial,
in orbit in the buckled sky,
a soul on its invisible

tether from the dippered
water that was self now
rise through the historical

ocean-skin that divides
the dreaming anchor from its days, each night
a nipped rehearsal for the unrequited

vessel filling in a child's
mind since the shock *unfair*
took it by force, unfairly into concept,

and Justice, signal star,
tore from its center to abide
above the ferns and shelters

where in dreams a life
soars up to lick the fabled light
from its inverted triangles, paired fairly in the sky,

glowing from our perspective
a phosphor that might nightly heal
the hole in the clay

flowerpot to brim
the unknown nourishment and balsamed,
angel with open eyes, untarred

and gleaming feathered, let
our solace be your
flight.

■

The visitors in room 8509
stand in a circle chanting something Russian.
The Hassids down the hall have come
in segregated silence, men
roll their thick white stockings in the lounge,
mother and sisters still
between the door and bed each time I pass.
We step across invisible or merely transparent
shadows making up their mind
to speak, to intervene, to cull.

A firm hand, like the a.m. nurse sponging the last
few hours of confusion
from the somehow childlike
emaciated limbs and face she lifts,
a bride, I swear, swathed in a sheet,
back on fresh linen and then clips
the bottoms of the flowers
keeping the family at bay while Barry naps
in her unbridled trust, we lack.
Not without prayer. Not without

the pluck and humor of the song
your bones thrum while the blood still laves
their broadside and their flank.
I kiss your bones. In mind
each rounded pinnacle
of rib is white
against an O'Keeffe sky and light
their lingua franca. Such thinking heals
the moment. It divides us
for its duration like a cyclone

fence from our despair, our rage, our bitter greedy fear.

■

The Masseuse

The friends of the dead lie on my table.
I do what I can
with their breath and my hands.
Witless, the birds are singing.
The crocus-garland month lengthens our light.
I want it
always to be light. I fight the night
and win. I peel my eye
against the black and white
T.V. until it dawns then sleep.
The Palestinian and Boston
homeless split the screen.
Number of children living on Brazilian streets.
What is forty million? Jeopardy's prey fill the camera
their stripped and stunning faces
emblazoned in the halogen
a kind of sustained lightning
and the peasant heart
who counts the seconds between flash
and fall of thunder shrinks
from the looming toll.
Horror is toxic.
The lesions
on our organs keep the score.
The gentle and the hard are being taken
in legions and the globe
might shake us off its flank like quarry dust
and start again with something less
free, less
wrecked by greed but it suffers us
on its blue cetacean patience
like festered barnacles.
Like counted sheep midair over a stream

the friends of the dead pause on my table.
The shophar is ringing like starlight
too young to have reached us.
I do what I can
with their breath and my hands.

■

MICHAEL BURKARD

almost to Jesus

almost to Jesus
the voices begin,
again the road
stumbles along with

the one walking it,
and walking it one makes
it, like a scene in
which the early light

is likened to the
walking stick of
an old maid or an
old man, two unto two—

the voices from the
town populace ring
as bells ring against
still cold noons:

& the sick are not to
be touched for they
are among us already
for they have wronged

and wronged us.
no one helps the old
who are young, or
anyone with the wrong

disease. & lights
of the nuclear base
burn on and out with
a monetary tinge, the

exact science of nuclear
sport receives more
homage than those already
dying. for this is as

always the beginning,
the end—a child walks
home to cure somebody,
the name is in the name

of no one. it is time
to help, it is time to
be help. like a scene
young, old, anyone's.

■

D e s e r t

for Ron

When we laugh in the desert
our voices are small pieces of paper.
We are alive, the papers say.

We don't know
anything but we can hear each other
when we are too small
to be seen, waving arms

so far away the swell of hill
and the half-buried monster
of rock almost inhaling

us asking from so
far away can you still
hear me I am alive.

You are alive
love   courage   words
like toy helmets   too
small for you

what kills
a second Ron
standing up in you
a gray child

you are alive
in that faith always
desert   sand blown into

places to stand
and see the world
that lasts is nothing.

■

KEVIN JEFFERY CLARKE

Kate

Your best friend
wrapped around the shroud
of his lover dying
from AIDS
with his mother also
holding him so peace
could circle each time
touching more lightly
so he could go on unassisted
into the new world
but for the mother-wheel
and lover-wheel to clear
a way for him and you know
he never believed it would
come for him with all its
pale promises and doors
left open so full of darkness
he never saw himself surrounded
by everything he loved
shining so finally
to make this last puzzled
and sorrowing picture
all the more so
he never saw any of that
in any distance.

■

The Rush to Ending

A cold fire sings in us

Is to touch you
to hand you the hereafter
in a huddle of heartline, mindline,
lines broken and still going on
and if you return the touch
is it to say what you tried in life
to say, that it still feels like, well, life,
but for the thorns and arterial blue and
the table setting and the shade always drawn
is every touch the last repeating itself
Narcissus smoothing his features
in a warehouse of water

To love the rage
of the male body
when it is lit
and the team of horses
it contains begins
to feel a rhythm like wind
return to them and the hair
is storm-loosened and the nacreous
buttons are methodically undone
and how in curving
a marriage to light begins
and a question faintly rises:
are we going to make it?

Last year a friend went dark
in a nervous city
alone, the sea flashing
against his glasses,
the sea sorted out at last

in his inner ear
so he could leave this world
as he'd entered it
through the undependable
irrational influence
of water

And a month back another friend
went out on an ordinary evening
with ordinary trees flowing
into his walking
and he stripped to work-out gear
and waited for the fountain of his body
to irrigate the dry stones
and left the gym and casually
fell into the street
the way a garden glove
would fall into a row of vegetables
to catch upon a thorn

The cold fire
The luggage stamped with final destinations
The blood driven monstrously off-course
The hard-won grace of men who died
loving so much, so hard, rudely,
on the open road, in orchard, on sloped roofs,
after long rains, in smoky railroad stations,
in time, in a hurry, no end to the rush to ending,
no flower harsher, more determined
than the human heart
as it pulls out of the contract
and sends down its astonished muscular roots
into earth,
the darker, truer address of all its music.

■

HENRI COLE

A Half-Life

There is no sun today,
save the finch's yellow breast,
and the world seems faultless in spite of it.
Across the sound, a continuous
ectoplasm of gray,
a ferry slits the deep waters,

bumping our little motorboats
against their pier.
The day ends like any day,
with its hour of human change
lifting even the choleric heart.
If living in someone else's dream

makes us soft, then I am so,
spilling out from the lungs
like green phlegm of spring.
My friend resting on the daybed
fills his heart with memory,
as July's faithful swallows

weave figure-eights above him,
vaulting with pointed wings and forked tails
for the ripe cherries he tosses them,
then ascending in a frolic
of fanned umbrella-feathers
to thread a far, airy steeple.

To my mind, the cherries form an endless
necklace-like cortex rising out
of my friend's brain, the swallows

unravelling the cerebellum's pink cord.
In remission six months, his
body novocained and irradiant,

he trembles, threadbare, as the birds unwheel him.
The early evening's furnace casts
us both in a shimmering sweat.
In a wisp Gabriel might appear to us,
as to Mary, announcing a sweet
miracle. But there is none.

The lilies pack in their trumpets,
our nesting dove nuzzles her eggs,
and chameleons color their skin with dusk.
A half-life can be deepened by the whole,
sending out signals of a sixth sense,
as if the unabashed, youthful eye

sees clearest to the other side.
A lemon slice spirals in the icy tea,
a final crystal pulse of sun reappears,
and a newer infinite sight
takes hold of us like the jet of color
at the end of winter. Has it begun:

the strange electric vision of the dying?
Give me your hand, friend.
Come see the travelers arrive.
Beneath the lazy, bankrupt sky,
theirs is a world of joy trancing
even the gulls above the silver ferry.

■

ROBERT CORDING

Elegy for John, My Student Dead of AIDS

In my office, where you sat years ago and talked
Of Donne, of how you loved
His persona, the bravado he could muster
To cover love's uncertainties,
Books still line the shelves, centuries
Of writers who've tried to make a kind of sense
Of life and death and, failing that,
Found words to stand at least
Against the griefs we can't resolve.

Now you're dead. And what I've got to say
Comes now from that silence
When our last talk fouled up. I allowed you less,
As always, than you wanted to say.
We talked beside the Charles, a lunch hour reunion
Of sorts after years of your postcards
(New York, San Francisco, Greece),
Failed attempts to find a place to live.
The warm weather had come on

In a rush. You talked of being the first born,
Dark-haired, Italian son. How you rarely visited
The family you so clearly loved.
I shifted to books, to sunlight falling
Through sycamores and the idle play of underlying
Shadows. When we parted,
All that was really left was the feeling
You deserved better. And yet I was relieved
Our hour was up, that we had kept your confusion

To yourself. We shook hands, you drove off to Boston.
Now you're dead and I wonder
If your nobleness of living with no one
To turn to ended in dishonor,
Your family ashamed. Or if your death had
About it a frail dignity,
Each darkening bruise precise as a writer's word,
Saying, at last, who you were—exactly
And to anyone who would listen.

■

ALFRED CORN

Assistances

Paris, London, Los Angeles—

men seated restlessly in a room
wait for clipped announcement of a name
grown faint and unfamiliar
to summon them upstairs.

The glare falling like cold enamel
on corked vials of venous blood,
each dyed with a message marked in code;
the dossiers that fatten
week by week, to whispered confidences
from white-clad figures in calm stances
conferring beyond the gauze of a curtain.

I think of you, friend and standard
bearer, first again to set out.
What can you not tell us about
the strong deliverance, the staggered
retreat of sound and sight,
loosing of the cord that bound
you to flesh, whose collapse still kept
a last function, the registry of pain?
Where yours ended, others take up
the relay, its sear and tremble at one
with hands that clasped, with hearts that leapt . . .
silent injunctions made to those who wait,
balancing between patience and complaint,
until you softly call their name.

■

Plague

When the world has become a pestilence,
a sullen, inexplicable contagion,

when men, women, children
die in no sense realized, in

no time for anything, a
painful rush inward, isolate—

as when in my childhood the
lonely leper pariahs so seemingly

distant were just down the street,
back of drawn shades, closed doors—

no one talked to them, no one
held them anymore, no one waited

for the next thing to happen—as
we think now the day begins

again, as we look for the faint sun,
as they are still there, we hope, and we are coming.

■

WILLIAM DICKEY

V i n d i c t i v e n e s s   o f   R e l i g i o n

It saddened me greatly to look at those twenty-three bright, shining, intelligent faces on the cover of the March San Francisco Focus *and realize that after their short time on earth, they'll all be spending the rest of eternity writhing in the fires of hell.*

Rev. John Thomas, San Jose

His tummy a
source of
fruit   waters of
refreshment

pilgrims oil   it
with their
headcloths are
beatified it
digests
them &

nothing   outside
nothing   dialogue
telephone curled
to the
womb-number nothing
interrupting
the
saved

   *

Crucifixus est   what
happens   demands
in its
adherents
replication the

                    meat   everywhere
                                bleeding being
        encouraged   bleeding being
                made
                to bleed

                                image of
                                stone at the
                    tomb's   mouth
                                        grinning

            the   tomb
                        opened &   empty but
                                        empty of
                                        nothing the
                    stone
                    having   won
        *
        Into his
                cincture of
                shadow   at
                                evening

                day was too
                much   the pain the
                        level   vision

        now they give up their   eyes what
                    illuminated
                                    the night
                                    slides it
                        is named
                hell   what
                                moves where
                                            waste
                    moves
                    stilling the
        living waters.
                        ■

DEBORAH DIGGES

Faith - Falling

Yes! My son has learned to fall by increments each day
backwards from the vaulting horse set just his height—
   his full weight—

into the broken bridge of arms extended by his classmates.
This means he'll trust the rope now that pins him to any
   mountain,

trust the least foothold, ice-slick, crumbling.
I like to imagine the times I've heard such cheers go up
   in school gymnasiums,

or stood, myself, at the cliff's edge, sounding, sounding.
I have a friend who taught me this week the work-a-day

of his disease, how not to sentimentalize his happiness—
in the morning radiation treatments, then lunch in the foothills,

where we spoke of the poem just out of reach, the one failed
   mostly, the one believed.
It's falling we do best, it's how we navigate the silence.

In the airplane on my way to him another passenger took snap-
   shots,
turned on her knees in her seat behind first class, aimed her
   camera to us all

and flashed and flashed. We smiled for her against the "chop,"
against the coffin-shaped fuselage, a hundred people, airsick,
   islanded, cresting

the thermals' high wakes, most of our dinner trays sent back
   untouched,
as from the dimmed rooms of a hospital. What could she hope
   for?

Surely the lighting's wrong, the angle foreshortening our faces,
already fear-blurred, bloated in the altitude.

Now somewhere in a darkroom, pinned frame by frame to the
   line,
we must look to be leaping out of ourselves,

like the Great Wallendas, who would have walked their doomed
high wire formations over Europe, if they could.

It must have looked so easy drawn out across the sand,
that stick-figure genealogy, that human pyramid suspended
   in the long shadows

of winter quarters, the sawdust smell domestic between trailers,
the big cats dozing in their cages, the apes grooming their
   young.

Then even the children were given bars to practice
on the low wires toward the moment they'd balance on their
   parents' shoulders,

balanced, without a net above the crowd.
When we touched down that night in California, we all applauded,

squeezed one another's hands. Terror had made us real enough
   to touch,
almost intimate, as we stepped from the jetway

flushed as performers from the wings,
and he was waiting. And he held me. On earth you can say goodbye.

■

Heartbeats

Work out. Ten laps.
Chin ups. Look good.

Steam room. Dress warm.
Call home. Fresh air.

Eat right. Rest well.
Sweetheart. Safe sex.

Sore throat. Long flu.
Hard nodes. Beware.

Test blood. Count cells.
Reds thin. Whites low.

Dress warm. Eat well.
Short breath. Fatigue.

Night sweats. Dry cough.
Loose stools. Weight loss.

Get mad. Fight back.
Call home. Rest well.

Don't cry. Take charge.
No sex. Eat right.

Call home. Talk slow.
Chin up. No air.

Arms wide. Nodes hard.
Cough dry. Hold on.

Mouth wide. Drink this.
Breathe in. Breathe out.

No air. Breathe in.
Breathe in. No air.

Black out. White rooms.
Head hot. Feet cold.

No work. Eat right.
CAT scan. Chin up.

Breathe in. Breathe out.
No air. No air.

Thin blood. Sore lungs.
Mouth dry. Mind gone.

Six months? Three weeks?
Can't eat. No air.

Today? Tonight?
It waits. For me.

Sweet heart. Don't stop.
Breathe in. Breathe out.

■

One by One

They won't go when I go.
Stevie Wonder

Live bravely in the hurt of light.
C.H.R.

The children in the life:
Another telephone call. Another man gone.
How many pages are left in my diary?
Do I have enough pencils? Enough ink?
I count on my fingers and toes the past kisses,
the incubating years, the months ahead.

Thousands. Many thousands.
Many thousands gone.

I have no use for numbers beyond this one
one man, one face, one torso
curled into mine for the ease of sleep.
We love without mercy.
We live bravely in the light.

Thousands. Many thousands.

Chile, I knew he was funny, one of the children,
a member of the church, a friend of Dorothy's.
He knew the Websters pretty well, too.
Girlfriend, he was real.
Remember we used to sit up in my house
pouring tea, dropping beads,
dishing this one and that one?
You got any T-cells left?

The singularity of death. The mounting thousands.
It begins with one and grows by one
and one and one and one
until there's no one left to count.

■

Yours free without the asking
Quick delivery via overnight male,
Special Handling, or ten-year incubation.
How I Lost 40 Pounds in Two Weeks

Cocktails of Perrier with a twist of AZT,
Bactrim broiled with bacon bits
Egg lipid quiche for brunch. Our tongues
ablaze on toast points in a soundless howl.
The most talented minds, the best bodies
of my generation going up in smoke.

Act now. Dial 1-800-I GOT-IT-2.
Our operators are standing by.
I have photographs to prove it:
Before and After and Passed Away.

■

R e t r o v i r

Turn
back oh man
and see how where you've come from
looks from here: the light-
filled leak of sunrise, drone
of morning's clarity and fleeting sense
of firm direction, lunch with wine,
siesta and the afternoon you're part of.
Here the sky is always blue
and white, the colors of the pills
that poison you while they extend your life,
inoculating you with time
that draws you back with fingers
curved around the bowstring.
You are not the target, you're the arrow
and the dirty wind that hits
your face on summer streets these
too-long evenings means you're moving
faster than you know, a shrill
projectile through the neutral air
above a world war, headed for the flesh
of someone's notion of croquet
at twilight on the lawn. The thickening
damp crowds out the light, as green
of grass and fountain separates
to blue and white.

■

T i a r a

Peter died in a paper tiara cut
from a book of princess paper dolls;
he loved royalty, sashes

and jewels. *I don't know,*
he said, when he woke in the hospice,
I was watching the Bette Davis film festival

on Channel 57 and then—
At the wake, the tension broke
when someone guessed

the casket closed because
"he was in there in a big wig
and heels," and someone said,

"You know he was always late,
he probably wasn't there yet—
he's still fixing his makeup."

And someone said he asked for it.
Asked for it—when all he did
was go down into the salt tide

of wanting as much as he wanted,
giving himself over so drunk
or stoned it almost didn't matter who,

though they were beautiful,
stampeding into him in the simple,
ravishing music of their hurry.

I think heaven is perfect stasis
poised over the realms of desire,
where dreaming and waking men lie

on the grass while wet blue horses
roam among them, huge fragments
of the music we die into

in the body's paradise.
Sometimes we wake not knowing
how we came to lie here,

or who has crowned us with these temporary,
precious stones. And given
the world's perfectly turned shoulders,

the deep hollows blued by longing,
given the irreplaceable silk
of horses rippling

in orchards, fruit thundering
and chiming down, given salt
and a tongue to long for it

and gravity, what could he do,
what could any of us ever do
but ask for it.

■

Turtle, Swan

Because the road to our house
is a back road, meadowlands punctuated
by gravel quarry and lumberyard,
there are unexpected travelers
some nights on our way home from work.
Once, on the lawn of the Tool

and Die Company, a swan;
the word doesn't convey the shock
of the thing, white architecture
rippling like a pond's rain—pocked skin,
beak lifting to hiss at my approach.
Magisterial, set down in elegant authority,

he let us know exactly how close we might come.
After a week of long rains
that filled the marsh until it poured
across the road to make in low woods
a new heaven for toads,
a snapping turtle lumbered down the center

of the asphalt like an ambulatory helmet.
His long tail dragged, blunt head jutting out
of the lapidary prehistoric sleep of shell.
We'd have lifted him from the road
but thought he might bend his long neck back
to snap. I tried herding him; he rushed,

though we didn't think those blocky legs
could hurry—then ambled back
to the center of the road, a target
for kids who'd delight in the crush
of something slow with the look
of primeval invulnerability. He turned

the blunt spear point of his jaws,
puffing his undermouth like a bullfrog,
and snapped at your shoe,
vising a beakful of—thank God—
leather. You had to shake him loose. We left him
to his own devices, talked on the way home

of what must lead him to new marsh
or old home ground. The next day you saw,
one town over, remains of shell
in front of the little liquor store. I argued
it was too far from where we'd seen him,
too small to be his . . . though who could tell

what the day's heat might have taken
from his body. For days he became a stain,
a blotch that could have been merely
oil. I did not want to believe that
was what we saw alive in the firm center
of his authority and right

to walk the center of the road,
head up like a missionary moving certainly
into the country of his hopes.
In the movies in this small town
I stopped for popcorn while you went ahead
to claim seats. When I entered the cool dark

I saw straight couples everywhere,
no single silhouette who might be you.
I walked those two aisles too small
to lose anyone and thought of a book
I read in seventh grade, *Stranger than Science*,
in which a man simply walked away,

at a picnic, and was,
in the act of striding forward
to examine a flower, gone.
By the time the previews ended
I was nearly in tears—then realized
the head of one-half the couple in the first row

was only your leather jacket propped in the seat
that would be mine. I don't think I remember
anything of the first half of the movie.
I don't know what happened to the swan. I read
every week of some man's lover showing
the first symptoms, the night sweat

or casual flu, and then the wasting begins
and the disappearance a day at a time.
I don't know what happened to the swan;
I don't know if the stain on the street
was our turtle or some other. I don't know
where these things we meet and know briefly,

as well as we can or they will let us,
go. I only know that I do not want you
—you with your white and muscular wings
that rise and ripple beneath or above me,
your magnificent neck, eyes the deep mottled autumnal colors
of polished tortoise—I do not want you ever to die.

■

B i l l ' s S t o r y

When my sister came back from Africa,
we didn't know at first how everything
had changed. After a while Anne
bought men's and boy's clothes in all sizes,
and filled her closets with little
or huge things she could never wear.

Then she took to buying out
theatrical shops, rental places on the skids,
sweeping in and saying, *I'll take everything.*
Dementia was the first sign of something
we didn't even have a name for,
in 1978. She was just becoming stranger,

all those clothes, the way she'd dress me up
when I came to visit. It was like we could go back
to playing together again and get it right.
She was a performance artist, and she did
her best work then, taking the clothes to clubs,
talking, putting them all on, talking.

It was years before she was in the hospital,
and my mother needed something
to hold on to, some way to be helpful,
so she read a book called *Deathing*
(a cheap, ugly verb if ever I heard one)
and took its advice to heart;

she'd sit by the bed and say, *Annie,
look for the light.* It was plain
that Anne did not wish to be distracted
by these instructions; she came to,
though she was nearly gone then, and looked
at our mother with what was almost certainly

annoyance. *It's a white light,*
Mom said, and this struck me
as incredibly presumptuous, as if the light
we'd all go into would be just the same.
Maybe she wanted to give herself up
to indigo, or red. If we can barely even speak

to each other, living so separately,
how can we all die the same?
I used to take the train to the hospital
and sometimes the only empty seats
would be the ones that face backwards.
I'd sit there and watch where I'd been

waver and blur out, and finally
I liked it, seeing what you've left
get more beautiful, less specific.
Maybe her light was all that gabardine
and flannel, khaki and silks
and stripes. If you take everything,

you've got to let everything go. Dying
must take more attention than I ever imagined.
Just when she'd compose herself
and seem fixed on the work before her,
Mother would fret, trying to help
just one more time—*Look for the light*—

until I took her arm
and told her wherever I was in the world
I would come back, no matter how difficult
it was to reach her, if I heard her calling.
Shut up, mother, I said, and Annie died.

■

CAROL EBBECKE

Good Timing

Fran, you lay belly up in a bed
with two side rails where it is impossible
for me to join you, the first thing
I noticed after I saw patches of hair
falling along the contour of your shoulders
falling from that incredible head

I wanted to hold it to my waist, thinking
maybe I could bring you into the world again,
some way, bring you from myself, where you might
find some softness apart from your growing
edges, growing sharp,

saying you'll never hate me, I who unknowingly
sought you, who inflicted this shitty virus,
my meaning to swallow you in lust, but now
in a wash of extra blankets, hot packs in a fever,

you're caught between one blanket sheet and another,
wrapped in a serial wrist bracelet not for fashion
but for life. For what's left I'm waiting
without surprise—or any sense of style, just waiting
for my own first loss of breath,

for sweat to come before, to be the only thing
that does, and you die away every day. You can't
keep returning for much longer, even in the dark
you don't fall without scarring anymore, no sighs
wanting, no goodbyes.

No posing on my part, no mistress, no angel waiting for
forgiveness for what she has and has forgotten today,
just knowing in the dark that patches fall back
into place, there is room in your bed, two rails
will hold us all night, and good timing
only touches but some.

■

F o r R i c h a r d

Your tears come
to you now
at once
like hungry dogs.
The world's on fire.
They keep taking away your future
like your driver's license.
They don't want you back on the road.
Statistics: live barbed wire
around your genitals.
And you, who no longer separate
the red heart
from the breaking one,
you, whose living they can't explain
you grow unmistakably
solidly round
like Buddha.

■

The Veteran

Even before the fear of blackmail and police,
being beaten up, strapped in for shock, and worse,
the humiliation of being dragged out into the open,

the boyscout manual promised
that it would drive us crazy,
which didn't keep me from uncontrollable
beating-off under the covers,
followed by dread.

The army kept showing a film of chancre sores,
raw meat penises, rotten tongues held out with forceps,
a guy who could only whisper hoarsely
for us not to make the mistake he did—
and a million times I was convinced
I caught something in every sneaky sex act.
Oh, the heart-sinking disgust
of coming up with a crab-louse in the tweezers,
pale legs in slow motion.

How could it not have come, then, to this,
the ultimate punishment of AIDS, an inner voice argues—
even while good sense says it's just a disease,
not a moral judgment.

Caught in crystal like a prehistoric insect
that lived but never quite flew,
the mineral hardening around him,
it's with regret, but truthfully also relief,
that this old veteran—masturbator, midnight stalker—
fed up with it from a lifetime of guilt and worry,
can at last put sex away, probably forever.

■

GARY FINCKE

The First AIDS Case in Selinsgrove

First, he said, he stepped
on something the river washed
here from the city, and then
it was like dandelions in him,
as if he'd been seeded.
From the bridge, he said,
you can see the shards
in the water and dream
yourself jumping, and
his story is following
the fishermen downstream,
and they are baiting
their lines with glass,
reeling in everyone
who is tempted by edges,
who swims toward them
with a kind of love.

■

The AIDS List

At breakfast, the AIDS list,
A magazine cover of faces;
On the front porch a possum
Half-grown and dead and my cat
Looking from kill to me before
Dodging *The People's Almanac*,
Heavy enough to make me killer,

Too, triple cruelty this morning,
Drawn to my doorway by the screams
Of schoolchildren. And I think
Chipmunk, rabbit, mouse, bird—
The slaughter list, something like
The ones on the flapped-open page:
20 Illegitimate Children;
12 People Who Disappeared
And were Never Found, though
Patty Hearst returned, I know,
And so will my cat with another kill,
Feathers or fur, gifts from the genes
Like DaVinci, Dumas, Strindberg, Wagner,
Four of the twenty love children,
The cat squalling its list
Of complaints from the shrubbery
As if research were as simple
As lust, as if it were insurance
For what we think we need to know.

■

ALLEN GINSBERG

Sphincter

I hope my good old asshole holds out
sixty years it's been mostly ok
tho in Bolivia a fissure operation
    survived the altiplano hospital—
a little blood, no polyps, occasionally
    a small hemorrhoid
active, eager, receptive to phallus
    coke bottle, candle, carrot
    banana & fingers—
Now AIDS makes it shy, but still
    eager to serve—
out with the dumps, in with the
    orgasmic friend—
Still rubbery muscular,
    unashamed wide opened for joy
But another 20 years who knows,
    old folks got trouble everywhere
necks, prostates, stomachs, joints—
    Hope the old hole stays young
    till death, relax

3/15/86—1 p.m.

Frozen Stiff

It's not that I'm wallowing
in it
but there is this lonely pond which
since it's January again
is frozen over thick, or not "over"
is itself frozen through and through
with green and yellow snot colors
like the shadows of beautiful trout
the shadows of a summer
and now walk walk
talk talk
we were smaller then than now
but still had much to say
and the knowledge of a dead boy
stiff as a stick
wedged somewhere below in the ice
behooves us to watch our step
to avoid the hairline crack which runs through
as a hairline minuscule crack in the skeleton
of a friend's foot
causes the young man to lie up in bed for a fortnight
and this is someone who "runs around all day"
I hope now to just keep on walking some
up over the hill
practically filled (like a clay cake) with old fossils
from prehistoric days and prehistoric nights.

Before the Ice Age
there was plenty of flora and fauna
the hills were a scramble of skin and breath
over past the meandering river

filled with prehistoric fishes
as big as bread boxes
and then everything slowed down again
(as it is doing this winter in my life)
and there was very little progress
across the meandering geography
there is so little time
to waste it by using the same word twice
"meandering"
or making the same mistake twice
or having a new friend who
it turns out is accident-prone
just like the last one
who ended up at the bottom of the solid pond
I'll never forget that boy I hardly knew
he (though) is like a sliver of scenery, a prop,
and in my lyric balance I would love to brag
I forgot, or escaped from,
the lugubrious dikes & shallows
that so bogged me down back then
but whose pressure *does*—
now we might go so far as to describe it as "self-indulgently"—
grow and grow
the more it stays the same.

■

DAVID GROFF

A Scene of the Crime

Going home near dawn from the last great party
Of the '78 season, where Miss Fire Island
Got a long drugged kiss from a Perry Ellis model,
He hears behind a slatted wooden fence
The suction of two men fucking.
Their sweat seems to moisten the dry air.
The ocean mutters, the men mutter
And laugh, a rhinestone bracelet
Sails gleaming toward the stars
Like a falling star until it sinks
With a careless plop into the pool.
He stands transfixed, lonely, high,
Unable to force himself away,
Smoking one, two, three cigarettes, awaiting
The usual, shrill, orgasmic cry.
It comes, and then, "Rog, I love you, I love you!"
One, two bodies dive into the pool and make a single
Splash that causes him to love the whole idea of love.

He drops his cigarette, forgets to scratch it out,
And heads home to his rented bed
Drunk with other people's sex,
Aware in other rooms and other houses, in the wild,
Of the salty come-togethers of some thousand men.
This odd domestic life—greased by drugs and easy-come,
Easy-go—goes on, so naturally, so left-alone.
Elsewhere, Sadat and Begin make their peace.
He falls asleep, glad for the flaming island.

Amazing how long a cigarette could burn.
Iran and Carter fall, Gloria bellows
At the island like a very mad contestant,
And late one fall, long after Reagan gets his way,
In the driest leaves occurs the slyest kind of arson:

An ember awakes to find itself a flame
And flames surprise themselves into a fire.
Above the brush, the boardwalk bursts
Into hunger so fierce it seems years in the making.
It gobbles the dune to the door, unsated, until
The house is a swift-collapsing pile of smoke
And microscopic sparks dance from roof to roof;
Men who are seasoned but unprepared for fire
Scuttle from house after house that burns and burns.
They inhale the ash of burning poison ivy.

The following spring, with the world's little wars
Torching a hundred here, another dozen there,
But with the national economy still fairly firm,
On a day so great the deer emerge
To eat the holly berries and nose the surf,
The man who didn't mean to
Walks the boardwalk once again, in sunlight, older.
When he finds the house a mass of twisted
Board and curtain rod and melted glass
He breathes in hard and feels in his lungs
The stink of fire.
He recalls his smoke and chokes with guilt—
But he considers how many years have passed
Since the night he thought he fell in love with love.
He considers then the usual comparison to AIDS
That sweeps his island like a fire,
An accident they seem to breathe.
At that moment on the island, in a thousand cities,
Another dozen soldiers in the fiercest war
Drop and collapse like stars,
Caught by the sniper.
He feels the bullets strike between their shoulder blades
And hears the groan as they go down.
He lights a cigarette, blows out the match,
And, feeling singed, stares at the pool
Braceleted by cyclone fence,
A crater filled with water and ash.
He wonders if they were lovers. Did the lovers burn?

The Reassurance

About ten days or so
After we saw you dead
You came back in a dream.
I'm all right now you said,

And it *was* you, although
You were fleshed out again:
You hugged us all round then,
And gave your welcoming beam.

How like you to be kind,
Seeking to reassure.
And, yes, how like my mind
To make itself secure.

■

The Man with Night Sweats

I wake up cold, I who
Prospered through dreams of heat
Wake to their residue,
Sweat, and a clinging sheet.

My flesh was its own shield:
Where it was gashed, it healed.

I grew as I explored
The body I could trust
Even while I adored,
The risk that made robust,

A world of wonders in
Each challenge to the skin.

I cannot but be sorry
The given shield was cracked,
My mind reduced to hurry,
My flesh reduced and wrecked.

I have to change the bed,
But catch myself instead

Stopped upright where I am
Hugging my body to me
As if to shield it from
The pains that will go through me,

As if hands were enough
To hold an avalanche off.

■

Terminal

(J.L., August '86)

The eight years' difference in age seems now
Disparity so wide between the two
That when I see the man who armoured stood
Resistant to all help however good
Now helped through day itself, eased into chairs,
Or else led step by step down the long stairs
With firm and gentle guidance by his friend,
Who loves him, through each effort to descend,
Each wavering, each attempt made to complete
An arc of movement and bring down the feet
As if with that spare strength he used to enjoy,
I think of Oedipus, old, led by a boy.

■

The Missing

Now as I watch the progress of the plague
The friends surrounding me fall sick, grow thin
And drop away. Bared, is my shape less vague
—Sharply exposed and with a sculpted skin

I do not like the statue's chill contour,
Not nowadays. The warmth investing me
Led outward through mind, limb, feeling, and more
In an involved increasing family.

Contact of friend led to another friend,
Supple entwinement through the living mass
Which for all that I knew might have no end,
Image of an unlimited embrace.

I did not just feel ease, though comfortable:
Aggressive as in some ideal of sport,
With ceaseless movement thrilling through the whole,
Their push kept me as firm as their support.

But death—Their deaths have left me less defined:
It was their pulsing presence made me clear.
I borrowed from it, I was unconfined,
Who tonight balance unsupported here,

Eyes glaring from raw marble, in a pose
Languorously part-buried in the block,
Shins perfect and no calves, as if I froze
Between potential and a finished work.

—Abandoned incomplete, shape of a shape,
In which exact detail shows the more strange,
Trapped in unwholeness, I find no escape
Back to the play of constant give and change.

■

To the Dead Owner of a Gym

I will remember well
The elegant decision
To that red line of tile
As margin round the showers
Of your gym, Norm,
In which so dashing a physique
As yours for several years
Gained muscle every week
With sharper definition.
Death, on the other hand,
Is rigid and,
Finally as it may define
An absence with its cutting line,
           Alas,
           Lacks class.

■

Still Life

(L.H., Dec. 5th, '86)

I shall not soon forget
The greyish-yellow skin
To which the face had set:
Lids tight: nothing of his,
No tremor from within,
Played on the surfaces.

He still found breath, and yet
It was an obscure knack.
I shall not soon forget
The angle of his head,
Arrested and reared back
On the crisp field of bed,

Back from what he could neither
Accept, as one opposed,
Nor, as a life-long breather,
Consentingly let go,
The tube his mouth enclosed
In an astonished O.

■

In Time of Plague

My thoughts are crowded with death
and it draws so oddly on the sexual
that I am confused
confused to be attracted
by, in effect, my own annihilation.
Who are these two, these fiercely attractive men
who want me to stick their needle in my arm?
They tell me they are called Brad and John,
one from here, one from Denver, sitting the same
on the bench as they talk to me,
their legs spread apart, their eyes attentive.
I love their daring, their looks, their jargon,
and what they have in mind.

Their mind is the mind of death.
They know it, and do not know it,
and they are like me in that
(I know it, and do not know it)
and like the flow of people through this bar.
Brad and John thirst heroically together
for euphoria—for a state of ardent life
in which we could all stretch ourselves
and lose our differences. I seek
to enter their minds: am I a fool,
and they direct and right, properly
testing themselves against risk,
as a human must, and does,
or are they the fools, their alert faces
mere deaths heads lighted glamorously?
I weigh possibilities
till I am afraid of the strength
of my own health
and of their evident health.

They get restless at last with my indecisiveness
and so, first one, and then the other,
move off into the moving concourse of people
who are boisterous and bright
carrying in their faces and throughout their bodies
the news of life and death.

■

MARILYN HACKER

---

for Lewis Ellingham

> *The laughing soldiers fought
> to their defeat*
> James Fenton,
> "In a Notebook"

White decorators interested in Art,
Black fileclerks with theatrical ambitions,
kids making pharmaceutical revisions
in journals Comp. instructors urged they start,
the part-Cherokee teenage genius—maybe—,
the secretary who hung out with fairies,
the copywriter wanting to know, where is
my husband? The soprano with the baby,
all drank draught beer or lethal sweet Manhattans
or improvised concoctions with tequila
in summer, when, from Third Street, we could feel a
night breeze waft in whose fragrances were Latin.
The place was run by Polish refugees:
squat Margie, gaunt Speedy—whose sobriquet
transliterated what? He'd brought his play
from Lodz. After a while, we guessed Margie's
illiteracy was why *he* cashed checks
and *she* perched near the threshold to ban pros,
the underage, the fugitive, and those
arrayed impertinently to their sex.
The bar was talk and cruising; in the back
room, we danced: Martha and the Vandellas,
Smokey and the Miracles, while sellers
and buyers changed crisp tens for smoke and smack.

Some came in after work, some after supper,
plumage replenished to meet who knew who.
Behind the bar, Margie dished up beef stew.
On weeknights, you could always find an upper
to speed you to your desk, and drink till four.
Loosened by booze, we drifted, on the ripples
of Motown, home in new couples, or triples,
were back at dusk, with I.D.'s, at the door.
Bill was my roommate, Russell drank with me,
although they were a dozen years my seniors.
I walked off with the eighteen-year-old genius
—an Older Woman, barely twenty-three.
Link was new as Rimbaud and better looking,
North Beach *paideon* of doomed Jack Spicer,
like Russell, our two-meter artificer,
a Corvo whose *ecclesia* was cooking.
Bill and Russell were painters. Bill had been
a monk in Kyoto. Stoned, we sketched together,
till he discovered poppers and black leather
and Zen consented to new discipline.
We shared my Sixth Street flat with a morose
cat, and arch cat, and pot-plants we pruned daily.
His boyfriend had left him for an Israeli
dancer; my husband was on Mykonos.
Russell loved Harold who was Black and bad,
and lavished on him dinners "meant for men"
like Escoffier and Brillat-Savarin.
Staunch blonde Dora made rice. When she had
tucked in the twins, six flights of tenement
stairs they'd descend, elevenish, and stroll
down Third Street, desultory night patrol
gone mauve and green under the virulent
streetlights, to the bar, where Bill and I
(if we'd not come to dinner), Link, and Lew,
and Betty had already had a few.
One sweatsoaked night in pitiless July,
wedged on booth-benches of cracked Naugahyde,
we planned a literary magazine

where North Beach met the Lower East Side Scene.
We could have titled it *When Worlds Collide.*
Dora was gone, "in case the children wake up."
Link lightly had decamped with someone else
—the German engineer? Or was he Bill's?
Russell's stooped *vale* brushed my absent makeup.
Armed children spared us home, our good-night hugs
laisser passer. We railed against the war.
Soon, some of us bussed south with SNCC and CORE.
Soon, some of us got busted dealing drugs.
The fileclerks took exams and forged ahead.
The decorators' kitchens blazed persimmon.
The secretary started kissing women,
and so did I, and my three friends are dead.

■

RACHEL HADAS

The Lenten Tunnel

You kneel and retch and pray,
gargle for help in the dark,
weak as a child. Unlike a child
in lowering your sobs
not to awaken the beloved sleeper,
you give the finger to what
blocks air, chokes you like a locomotive.

You last the darkness out.
Not quite dawn yet, but night
exhausted, colors seep
back into bed and table,
into M's sleeping face,
into your arms, your hands,
and finally the mirror,

the specter through whose terror
you daily find the strength
to put yourself together,
your own familiar gaze
piercing the patchy pallor.
Morning. The child whose dreams
I'm privileged to hear

told me today a comet,
luminous, streaming, last night
filled the sky of his sleep.
You say the end of your tunnel
brims with radiance.
Whatever flows, I answer,
must have found a channel.

■

JOSEPH HANSEN

Red Suspenders,
Boxes of Cigars

I'm wrong and know I'm wrong but can't help think
it's about time you telephoned again.
You'll never telephone again. You're dead.
Along toward the end, when you were wondering
why no amount of pills could kill the pain,
you couldn't work and couldn't pay your bill,
I couldn't phone you: had to wait your calls.
You borrowed five hundred bucks from me and then
five hundred more and yet your phone kept still.
You looked strange on those visits in your red
suspenders, but you lied blithely, said
you had a job, not that you'd soon be dead.
Your calls, desperation only half concealed in jokes
too quickly rattled off, began to come
from pay phones in the night. To say you'd pay
me back, honest you would—starting next week.
And you were dying and you never said so.
What a pathetic game you chose to play,
the rules your secret, all of us blind and dumb.
Then the calls came from hospitals, where everything was fine one day, and the whole staff
crazy the next. You couldn't pull yourself
awake to sign a paper. You rang for the nurse
at eight-thirty at night to help you to
the washroom. You came out, she saw you back to
bed again, you sighed and closed your eyes
and died. I miss your jokes. In your junk heap
of an apartment, nothing seemed funny.
Boxes of cigars in closets, under tables. Nothing
seemed funny. Bolo knives. A list of records.

They were awful jokes. You were too loud. You
lied, rarely paid anyone back his money.
I'm wrong and know I'm wrong, but can't help wish
you'd visit me again, choosing the worst
of times, as you always did, volleying laughter,
banging your beer can, spilling cigar ashes,
wanting something, always wanting something.
I couldn't spare you. Phone me any time.

■

The Dolphins

Who hasn't
at some point
succumbed.
Their sleek
intelligence
their wit.
The charm of a
boy on a dolphin.

Since men first tried the
dark oceans, these silver mammals
have burst into the blue air
unexpected as friendship.
And lonely sailor boys
might strip to imitate
the sport these brothers took
in each other's shining bodies.

In the dark caves
behind the bars
pretty boys
beautiful men
still swim in their
pleasure like dolphins
at death in the seas.

Nothing avails their
animal innocence.
Extinction is the
unnatural act.

The dolphin's song
fades like the ocean
noise trapped in a
conch shell, the last
shy smile of a
boy drowned at sea.

■

The Enticing Lane

If I should be told,
suddenly and quite unceremoniously,
that I too had
The Disease and would be taken
from all this,
I would think over the years,
I had complained too much—
the phone's ringing constantly
(lucky I was to have
so many friends),
the hours of my job
(fortunate I was to have
a job I liked),
the lover leaving
(ah, but he was here,
wasn't he, and in my arms
for so long?).
I should have lived in
the moment, kept a secret
corner for myself to breathe in,
allowed my life to blossom
at last—each leaf uncurling
wet with secrecy to dry
in the spring air.
I should have taken more risks—
old stick-in-the-mud that I am—
a balloon trip over the estuary;
speaking up on behalf of the
deaf-mute man at the bank who
was so rudely abused by the teller;
that antique bowl with red

peonies on it that I could
have bought in a shop in England.
But I let myself be dissuaded
by the sensible people.
I should have sought more balance—
silence/laughter,
cool shadow/hot rain,
nights drunk on someone/nights
alone with the dark's quiet watching.
I should have followed intuition
to the Nth degree and trusted it,
kept to that singular path, the enticing
lane with plush hedges, ripe fruit
and wafting scents that is always there
in the heart's eye and I could have
walked it, always prepared,
even into Death's Unknown and
still have been content, peaceful
as a child dawndreaming by open windows
before the others are up and everyone,
even the child, is wrenched into the world's
bombardment, the maelstrom of appointments
which constitutes a life.

■

Begging the Question

Fatal, to put the end before the means,
Similarly futile to regret
Those dinosaurs and obsolete machines
Of pleasure one can never quite forget.

Polymorphous as a Hindu god,
Pain has many faces, arms and legs
Innumerable. Infinitely odd
The unanswerable questions that it begs.

■

Unhappy Returns

With all the sinister abruptness of
Involuntary memory in Proust
Imaginative flights return to roost;
Sudden and insidious as love,

The telephone's coercive, tinny laugh
Interrupts and thus defines an idyll,
Peremptorily bringing in the middle
Of a meal, a nap, a paragraph

Word of a law-suit or a legacy,
Congratulations, gossip and complaint,
And, yesterday, a minatory, faint
Voice, "It's Nemesis—remember me"

■

EDWARD HIRSCH

And Who Will Look
Upon Our Testimony

On an unsuspecting Wednesday in October 1347,
       A Genoesan crew
  "Who had sickness clinging to their very bones"
    Brought the black rats and fleas
Flooding into the Messina harbor
          On the Northeast coast of Sicily.

The twelve galleys that landed had been driven
       By fierce winds
  From the East, infected and laden with spices.
    In three days the known world
Was changed forever by children
         Vomiting blood and howling for light.

It was changed by young Sicilian fishermen
      Who ran through town
  Screaming about the boils swelling in their
    Groins and under their armpits
Like blistering almonds,
        Like rotting eggs or apples.

The brackish blotches seethed and spread,
      Oozing blood and pus
  Until they turned into fiery purple knobs
    And peas sprouting on the arms,
Brittle black sea coals
        And cinders burning under the skin,

So that the stricken began to shiver and dance
          In strange bodily fits.
     Soon people were falling down in convulsions,
          Whirling through the streets
In a grim trance, and dying
                    In the terrible ecstasy of fever.

A mother saw the face of death seated on the face
          Of her startled daughter,
     A father saw the emeralds of death glowing
          In his son's eyes. The doctors believed
That one coughing child
                    Could infect the world's bloodstream,

And within months the continent was so bewildered
          And stupefied by pain
     That fathers abandoned their children, and wives
          Escaped from their husbands, brothers
Turned away from their sisters,
                    And mothers denied their sons.

Peasants fled from their cramped hamlets and towns,
          Leaving the wheat uncut
     And the harvest untended, the sheep roaming
          Aimlessly through the countryside
Until they, too, collapsed and
                    Died in the ditches and hedgerows.

Some people imagined a black giant striding
          Across the land,
     Others saw the Fourth Horseman of the Apocalypse.
          Some believed the plague had descended
In a rain of serpents and scorpions
                    When sheets of fire fell on the earth.

There were misty clouds, hot winds from the South.
                    A column of fire
Twisted above the papal palace of Avignon,
          And in Venice the tremoring earth
Set the bells of St. Mark's pealing
                    Without being touched by calloused hands.

The dancing went on. There were places where
                    "No one was left
To bury the dead, for money or friendship,
          And whole villages scattered, like dust
To the wind." No one mourned,
                    Nor did the death bells toll.

"In Siena great pits were dug and piled deep
                    With the multitude of dead.
And they died by the hundreds, nay, thousands,
          Both day and night, night and day,
And all were thrown into ditches
                    And covered up with the earth.

The people said and believed, *This is the end
                    Of the world!*
Blessed are those who did not witness
          The horror." Blessed are those
Who never fell victim to
                    The dancing mania and the stupor.

The Welsh sang of death coming into their midst
                    Like black smoke,
Like a rootless phantom who cuts down the young
          And shows no mercy to the fair.
*Woe is me of the shilling
                    And the black pest in the armpit!*

A clergyman recorded the death of five thousand sheep
In one field alone,
"Their bodies so corrupted from the plague
That neither beast nor bird
Would touch them." Preying wolves
Fled to the safety of the wilderness.

Some danced to the sound of drums and trumpets,
Fighting the ghost
With the high jollity of a happy music.
Some kept carefully unto themselves,
Barricaded into their homes,
Avoiding the grasp of the Evil One.

The Pistoian merchants decided the Dance of Death
Was a warning from Heaven
About crooked businessmen from Pisa and Lucca,
The Circassian slaves thought the spots
Growing on their hands and necks
Were a punishment from their masters.

And in the country the peasants died grotesquely
On the roads
And in the fields. In the cities, the rich
Fled and the poor died in burrows.
"And everywhere men and women
Wandered around as if mad."

The people believed that the boils were God's
Tokens and stamps.
In April, some friars saw the Star of Pestilence
Exploding in the sky after Vespers;
In May, some nuns saw the Angel
Of Death rising over the steeples.

And still the corpses kept piling up in the streets
And the stench was foul.
In Paris, five hundred bodies a day were carried
In a procession of open carts
From the Hotel Dieu
To the cemetery of the Holy Innocents.

"And in these days was burying without sorrowe and
Wedding without friendschippe."
Priests bolted themselves inside of churches
And died alone. And penitents in sackcloths
Wound through the streets
Imploring the mercy of the Virgin

And hoping to appease Divine Wrath by sprinkling
Themselves with ashes,
By carrying candles and relics to the churches,
By tying ropes around their necks
And tearing out their hair
In acceptance of chastisement from Heaven.

The flagellants believed that God was punishing
The world for its sins,
And they roamed from town to town chanting
Hymns and wearing cowled white robes
Emblazoned with red crosses.
Some carried iron crosses in penance.

The martyrs gathered in a thick human circle
In the town square;
They stripped and scourged their naked torsos
With leather whips tipped with spikes
While the townsmen followed,
Groaning and sobbing in sympathy

And crazed women smeared the blood on their faces.
Across Central Europe
They were greeted as the frenzied redeemers
Of Christ the Tiger, Christ
The Avenging Angel, who rose up
And put his sword on their shoulders.

Soon they were rushing for the Jewish quarters,
Trailed by citizens
Howling for revenge and shrieking for blood.
And thus began the lynchings
And the slaughter of innocents
For poisoning wells and corrupting air.

Who will hear the testimony of eleven Savoy Jews
Who were burned alive
For carrying poison in narrow leather bags?
Who will hear the cries of the Basel Jews
Who were burned in wooden houses
That were built on an island in the Rhine?

At Speyer, the bodies of the murdered were piled
In great wine casks
And then sent cascading down the river.
On February 14, 1349, two thousand
Jews of Strasbourg were burned
In staked rows in the burial ground.

The four hundred Jews of Worms preferred to set
Themselves on fire.
And the Jews of Narbonne and Carcassonne
Were dragged out of their homes
And thrown into the flames.
No one listened to their cries.

"God is deaf now-a-days and deigneth not hear us."
The chronicler said,
"Things which should be remembered forever
Perish with time and vanish
From the memory
Of those who come after us."

The flagellants too dispersed, like night phantoms.
And now no one believes
That death is a black dog with a sword in its paws
Or that pestilence darts from the eyes
Or that a Pest Maiden emerges
From the lips in a clear blue flame

And flies from victim to victim. No one lights
Smoke pots against her visit,
Or falls down in terror before the wrathful God
Of the leper and the bloated sheep,
The corrupted bodies lying
In state for the starving dogs.

No one sings for the men and women who wandered
The world in madness
Or for the ghostly ships with their dead crews
Or for the chronicler who died
In the middle of an un-
Finished sentence about the plague:

"In the midst of this pestilence, there came
To an end . . ."
Fortunate are those who come afterward,
The unfallen inheritors of earth
Who turn away from the Dance
Of Death dying in the mind.

"Oh happy posterity who will not experience
Such abysmal woe—
And who will look upon our testimony
As fable." Oh happy posterity
Who will die in its own time
With its own wondering tales of woe.

■

WALTER HOLLAND

Petrarch

The Pines, Fire Island—1988

Years shaped like the tree trunks,
calligraphies of grey, teal and umbre;
the cross-marks for all our failed imaginings
and a friend's death.

The morning is green.
The house in the Pines—
flat squares and planks.

The birds sing like Petrarch,
their sonnets,
floating like letters of light—
lost missives of a humanist,
from the other end of the marsh.

We ascend the dunes,
a vantage to see
this illuminated page of sea.
Beyond summer homes,

a renaissance of blue—
an empty frame of beach.
When Laura died he wrote farewell
on parchment as thin and dry
as this air—

the face remembered
in a small tangle of words,
like the thicket we passed on the way home—
bunched-up, hidden, dark.

■

LYNDA HULL

Hospice

Frayed cables bear perilously the antiquated lift,
all glass and wrought-iron past each apartment floor
like those devices for raising and lowering
angels of rescue in Medieval plays. Last night
the stairwell lamps flickered off and I was borne up
the seven floors in darkness, the lift a small lit

cage where I thought of you, of the Catholic souls
we envisioned once, catechism class, the saint
in her moment of grace transfigured as she's engulfed
in flames. The lift shivered to a halt above the shaft
and I was afraid for a moment to open the grille,
wanting that suspension again, the requiemed hum

of one more city going on without me—Cockney girls
with violet hair swirling among the businessmen
and movie ushers of Soho, sullen in their jackets.
All of them staving off as long as they can
the inevitable passing away, that bland euphemism
for death. But I can't shake this from my mind:

your face with its hollows against hospital linen.
Newark's empty asylum wings opened again this year
for the terminal cases. Each day another
strung-out welfare mother, the streetcorner romeos
we used to think so glamorous, all jacked-up
on two-buck shots. It was winter when I last was home

and my mother found you on her endless dietician's
rounds, her heavy ring of keys. It was winter
when I saw you, Loretta, who taught me to curse
in Italian, who taught me to find the good vein
in the blue and yellow hours of our sixteenth year
among deep nets of shadows dragged through evening, a surf

of trees by the railway's sharp cinders. Glittering
like teen dream angels in some corny AM song,
buoyed by whatever would lift us above the smouldering
asphalt, the shingled narrow houses, we must
have felt beyond all damage. Still what damage carried you
all these years beyond the fast season of loveliness

you knew before the sirens started telling your story
all over town, before the habit stole
the luster from your movie starlet hair.
Little sister, the orderlies were afraid to
touch you. Tonight, the current kicks the lights
back on and there's the steady moan of the lift's

descent, the portion of what's left of this day spread
before me—stockings drying on the sill, the cool
shoulders of milk bottles—such small domestic salvations.
There was no deus ex machina for you, gone now
this half year, no blazing seraphim, finally
no miraculous escape, though how many times

I watched you rise again and again from the dead:
that night at the dealer's on Orange Street, stripping
you down, overdosed and blanched against the green linoleum,
ice and saline. I slapped you and slapped you until
the faint flower of your breath clouded the mirror.
In those years I thought death was a long blue hallway

you carried inside, a curtain lifting at the end
in the single window's terrible soft breeze where
there was always a cashier ready to take your
last silver into her gloved hands, some dicey, edgy game.
Beneath the ward clock's round dispassionate face
there was nothing so barren in the sift from minute

to absolute minute, a slow-motion atmosphere dense
as the air of Medieval illuminations with demons
and diaphanous beings. I only wished then
the cancellation of that hungering that turns us
towards the mortal arms of lovers or highways
or whatever form of forgetfulness we choose.

Your breath barely troubled the sheets, eyes closed,
perhaps already adrift beyond the body, twisting
in a tissue of smoke and dust over Jersey's
infernal glory of cocktail lounges and chemical plants,
the lonely islands of gas-stations lining the turnpike
we used to hitch towards the shore, a moment

I want back tonight—you and me on the boardwalk,
the casino arcade closed around its pinball machines
and distorting mirrors. Just us among sea-serpents,
those copper horses with mermaid's tails, porpoise fins,
and the reckless murmur of the sea. Watching stars
you said you could almost believe the world arranged

by a design that made a kind of sense. That night
the constellations were so clear it was easy
to imagine some minor character borne up
beyond judgment into heaven, rendered purely
into light. Loretta, this evening washes
over my shoulders, this provisional reprieve.

I've been telling myself your story now for months
and it spreads in the dusk, hushing the streets, and there
you are in the curve of a girl's hand as she lights
her cigarette sheltered beneath the doorway's plaster
cornucopia. Listen how all along the avenues trees
are shaken with rumor of this strange good fortune.

■

GREG JOHNSON

The Foreign Element

And so briefly we detained him in the hall,
asked Why? Why?—not using even that word
but only the kind of shell-shocked glare
these medical veterans dread, especially near
dinner time. Sighing, he faced a quick-witted blond aunt
and two blond cousins, a gaunt lover with rings
under his eyes, and three others lacking acknowledged
relevance or rank (we took turns delivering coffee)—
yet at least the mother lay resting, in a spare bed
downstairs. "Think of it," he said, again,
"as a foreign element in the blood, against which we have
no defenses." Giddy with sorrow, I thought
We have no defenses, yes we have no bananas,
as he added, impossibly, "We're doing all we can."

The aunt, whom I'd gotten to know and dislike,
marched back to Intensive Care when the white-coat
left, heels clattering like an infant's drums
as if *she'd* defend him, by God, but then stopped short
and threw herself in a nearby chair. The cousins
attended her new display of grief, while the lover
wandered off without meeting anyone's eyes
and we three milled without aim, as usual, becoming
foreign ourselves in this timeless fluorescent world
where the random invaded bodies came to die. Later,
we'd draw straws to see who would bear
the nightly non-news to his mother downstairs, recalling
all the way down
that in old times, when they killed
their messengers, words had a harsh, consoling power,

surging in the blood and cruelly expressed
in that thrilling reprimand.
Now, speaking a foreign language, we stare
at one another, useless, as we await another death
with its casual pomp and non-dramatic flair,
its message we don't dare to understand.

■

JUNE JORDAN

Poem for Buddy

Dedicated to Andre Morgan

In that same beginning winter
when the rains strained all credulity
swallowed highways
rolled mountains of mud down
mountains
buried boundaries
left 20,000 families homeless

In that same beginning winter
of the rivers rising up
some of the people rose
organic
secretly
out loud
and irresistible

in that same beginning winter
of the gods asleep and
rain
rain
rain
flood
mudslide and
the powerful at large and
lies
lies
lies
the rivers burst torrential
to attack to overcome
the limitations of all compromise

In that same beginning winter
when Duvalier and Marcos
fell into the torrents
streaming full and efflorescent out
between the blank walls and the sea
streaming aboriginal
as female

when the ku klux klan
the Duck Club and other crackpot
rah-rah
butchered Charles and Annie Goldmark
in Seattle
hung Timothy Lee
from a California weed tree
and captured two top nominations
in the state of Illinois

when Reagan reigned
from the Gulf of Sidra to the asinine appeal
of right-to-life
explosives and war-mongering
cut-backs on the already alive

when the great lakes trembled
when volcanos shook
when the desert flowers failed
when the farmers lost the land
when the Challenger blew up
when the Chairman of the Board skipped lunch

when the rain the lies lies lies
and the rain
and the rain
when the rivers burst torrential
to attack to overcome
the limitations of all compromise

from Pretoria to Port-au-Prince
from Manila to Managua
from the hanging tree for Timothy Lee
to Washington D.C.
when the rivers burst torrential

it was then that
in Manhattan
one Black homosexual
in a gym
by himself
he turned to the taunting cocksure
multitude of forty-five
miscellaneous straight men preoccupied by musculature
and scores of conquest
tight men tight against gay
rights gay everything around them gay
hey/whatever happened to
dictatorship
anyway
next thing you know and your dog will be gay
and your wife and the cop on the corner gay gay
teachers in the classroom gay
victims of aids gay soldiers
in uniform gay fathers
of children gay
athletes on the U.S. Olympic teams
of whatever gay
members of the city council gay
lovers who love themselves gay
mothers gay
brothers-in-law gay
nuns gay priests gay
gay T.W.A. pilots gay
lumberjacks
gay rockstars gay
gay revolutionaries they

were saying, "Enough
enough!"
when he
in the gym
by himself
this Black homosexual this man
took on the question: *If not here then where*
                      If not now—
And he spoke to them saying:
"Okay! Look at me!" And in front of them he stood
thinking
they should march into a stadium
and gathering there by the hundreds
tear out their eyes
that they may no longer see
me/this despicable growing minority
here
outside but gathered as strong as we stand.
They should tear out their eyes
so the world will look only
the way they believe to be
beautiful!
Because
we are everywhere
gay
and today you just can't be sure
anymore
who's who
or
what's what
now
can you?

But they did not move they
did not say anything and they broke
into the locker of this Black homosexual this
human being and they broke they smashed his glasses

that let him deal
real
among the gay and the grim
and he left that gym
by himself

In that same beginning winter
when the first rivers burst torrential
to attack to overcome
the limitations of all compromise

he slipped into the rising up
we who will irreversibly see
and name our own destiny
with our own
open eyes

■

ARNIE KANTROWITZ

At a Queen's Funeral

Well, she's gone, and
it looks like we are the experts
on death now, Miss Thing,
even though we thought we'd camp
for all eternity.

My dear, I'm sorry, but
you still look fabulous in black.
With all our widowhood,
we must know
more about how to wear mourning
than our mothers learned in that tacky war.

We must know
how to see through the dark
when the light goes out
in yet another sister's eyes
and how to look behind the lies—
like that perpetual boy in the wedding gown,
flashing a grin at his skull-faced groom.

What we don't know is
why we are still here dishing,
even though it's clear
this party's over and
it looks like a perfect time for us to go.

■

X. J. KENNEDY

For Jed

It wastes us all, Jed, you
More quickly than the rest.
Posted in your ward bed,
You watch carnations fail

In the tumbler of water we
Freshen, although you seldom
Ask for a drink. You front
A Great Ming Wall of boredom,

Battling at chess with Katz,
The cancerous pants-presser,
You hoist lance for your knight
While, outdoors, evening hovers

Like poisoned doves. Stand guard
On your state of quilted covers.
No one, nobody human
Stays immune forever.

■

MICHAEL KLEIN

Positive

So now you know how blood tricks life.
I don't mean cold. The blue slipping out of
Laguna's deepest echo is cold; the Laguna
of more air that you say will take you
clear out of Long Beach by the first.

Kevin, the summer we worked on 3rd Ave.
clinched us. You always came up
with something funnier, I read the next book
you saw the next movie, someone loved a man
who did not love them back.

Someone took the deciding right turn
down 30th St. past the psychiatric hospital
into other country for one weekend
of stormbringing peace, less than not, brutal.
We were envelopes opening each other

For more news, notices falling out
and ads for health. We knew where our forces
were taking us and not many people
were getting sick then. We'd hear about one,
maybe two—men only met once

—Laughed with, gave a direction to. Men,
brief as lights going out on a sign.
We could always take the day's full dose:
our cities, up to us—yours western,
more musical—mine, dissonant, less accurate.

Each one still a home to most of the men
fatigued, then wet, then out.
But Kevin, you're not sick yet.
You're a blood sample that can't decide
on rest or havoc. Right?

Diagnosis. The word shivers with its own
future in it. Denial likes the other word, prognosis
like the family doctor—a short car-trip
into town— I can remember my brother and I
singing "Angels": "Dr. Prognosis will see you now."

Diagnosis is that bold arrow on a map
at the elevator: "You are here."
And so I am, I am here.
And I don't know what will save you
or what will save me. I don't know what will keep me

From a less intensifying chill as each report
comes in, as each statistic lingers
to enact its monstrous number of blood
gripping memory, gripping fact-finding cell.
I just know that in another life

We might have been lovers,
a life pre-diagnosis, a life where there'd
be enough wood for a fire, enough time
to tell you how a rough day became steadied
with part thought, part dream.

I just know that as far east as I'll get,
I am sending you light.
I am keeping a story activated, I am leaving
the door, the spilling of danger in a good neighborhood,
the Christmas photograph of Jeff and you

And I dressed for a dance—Jeff: negative,
Kevin: positive, Michael: God knows—
a 10-pound book of fairy tales
a man gave me for taking him into the woods
the crystal that hangs over the bathroom mirror

Like a pendulum too charged with inner light
to move (a gift you gave me for getting
us out of traffic), the poems on AIDS
that are strewn on my desk
like notes from a difficult class,

The space heating, the little pool
of kids next door wishing and winning summer
into early October, the note you left
on one of your visits: to "Ochre,
love Kizzy."

The washing machine that will only spin
at the tail end of a delicate cycle,
the phone I will pull
out of the wall every time,
because when I am talking, I am cooking.

The sleep with you in Washington
the morning of the march of the radical faeries,
the nostalgic edgelight of an afternoon
gilding Georgetown architecture,
the eggs florentine, the secret but proud

Ownership of semen stains on black satin,
pink flannel sheets, the dry flowers disintegrated
on everything paper, the tear in the roof
of the loft that hasn't stretched out
into enough wet nights to harm us,

The last step that leads into it, where you pause
and the temperature changes for the good
because you're in, you're home.
I just know that I'm leaving all of these things
open, Kevin, open enough for the two of us to enter.

■

W h o l e   L i v e s   M i s s i n g

The strongest August sun
has set and jittery
March has handed you
a story
about your blood.

I know nothing about you
except the sex
we had—never wanted
to know
and poor baby,

it's what I remember.
Let's face it—
you're probably
going to die
and I'm furious at you,

at AIDS, at New York
taking its strange
long cue
from Calcutta.
Leaving St. Vincent's,

I passed the school
I went to.
I was a crazy talking picture
and I thought
I'd live through anything.

Who didn't?
Dysfunctional families
or not,
it seemed we had
only to get through

a sixties
of being handed
Kennedy's killing.
It was
the strongest story

that eked
through rationale
and right now
I can still hear
Gary Orin's girlish laughter,

still see
the sun
punching through holes
of an algae-green
window shade

almost 3:00
light spreading
into a schoolroom newsreel
of a death as elegant
as it is horrifying:

car radial
like a diamond needle,
the chauffeur
eerily bathed
in his own

lucky break of sun,
an arrow nervously floating
to a book depository
and the buzzwords

hatching:
motorcade,
incumbent,
acted
alone.

And as if history
could stop at just one killing
Oswald breaks from a power line
taking one final meteor
to the stomach—

whole lives missing.
The slow
repositioning
of the camera
from sun to blood. To sun.

■

Naming the Elements

for The Names Project
San Francisco, California

The names of the dead
are messages on black marble
and plunge into the earth.

They are the notes
of a war
we imagined forgetting.

What remains is how
things began: the naming—a linear
code narrowing—"Vietnam Veteran."

Names find light to later
circle grass.
It is 1:00 A.M. in Washington

a cursory wind version of October
keeps finding
Kennedy's flame

enlarging and reducing
as if his part of the world
were trying to rise

to the reluctant surface
of a lake.
I am thinking of the names for water.

Michael, I am floating into the next
morning of another life
into a white and burgeoning sun

rising behind a sobering capitol
unshakable as any other building
that forms the hinge

of this country dying.
The names of the AIDS dead
struggle through a hardening

sound system and land
like brass phoenixes in snow.
I cannot remember the names

of the living
until I have left out
the names of the dead.

We are all made of
our own people
laying names on the ground

like men unfurling the
video flag on the moon.
I am thinking of the names for earth.

I know what you mean
when you say a name
signals a whole neighborhood,

a family, a system of stars.
What gets left to us
this morning

is the serial enunciation
of names wanting to stay,
of wanting to name something.

Each panel of each name
enters my head
like the staccato

report from a full magazine.
I am thinking of the names for fire.
The day tries to keep ending.

When I think of one name I remember
another.
When I watch men of this city

dancing away the diagnosis—alone until
gratified—
I try not to see them

with names,
I try to see them
as intentions of light.

I try hearing them as sounds.
I cannot bear having to remember
them. Their names.

Once I move toward the marble dance floor
I am falling away.
I am the names for

my own dying as
I am thinking of names
for the air.

■

WAYNE KOESTENBAUM

The Answer Is in the Garden

I wanted proof of God's hunger, but no sacrifice
   Had tempted Him to eat for a thousand years.
I laid a Kleenex on my windowsill for altar
   And offered the Sweet-Tarts that I'd shoplifted.
Waking to find my candy there and slightly dusty,
   I struck back by wasting the Sabbath in bed
Blindly stumbling through *Nietzsche and Christianity:*
   Its language was impossible, but I wished
My parents to know that I'd been abused by the powers.
   I don't mean this to be a dull history
Of my reading life, but what I'm drawn to say begins
   With a book that like a trick of light opened
The subject of death which I have not the power to close—
   I must begin with *The Supernatural*'s
Infra-red pictures of London witch covens dancing,
   Nude men and women with cellulite bellies
That looked pregnant—for a man is said to be pregnant
   When he sees the future like a charcoal sketch
Rising from the undrawn. The book showed dimes on shut eyes
   Of possessed Caribbeans, and a dead boy
Knocking on a door for centuries—the runaway
   I dreamed peered into my room because he was
Exiled by his Lancastrian parents and had need
   Of delinquent's shelter. Would I let him break
My window open? I'd read about his court ordeal
   In a scholastic magazine, a special
Issue about the other world: the story promised
   A sequel that never came, and the years passed
With the boy stationed eternally outside my room
   Inquiring if I were generous enough
To offer my floor to his thorn-scarred back. A lost boy
   Whom circumstance has reduced to trespassing,

With soot face he implores me through the window, and knows
  That after supper, when trees howl, there will be
Time for us to conspire. I can't dismiss such stories.
  In Michigan, a haunting light never left
A lakeside mansion: the red glow behind the rose-bush
  Watched the daughter study her geography
And the chandelier fell on the dining room table
  Just as lights had crashed one century ago
On the late master's head. *De riguer* campfire fables—
  Bermuda Triangle, Kennedy death plots—
Touched me as only the watery, unrigorous
  Mind can be shaken: of my epiphanies
I demand little more than an impression of speed,
  Illusion that I am moving toward an end
Unseen by all but the wisest spectators, who look
  Not for real prophecy, but the skeleton
Of enchantment, private auguries, a ringing phone.

  Omens come in series. Their recitation
Takes its toll, my legs feel weak. At the airport we saw
  A lean man—attractive, consumptive, or just
Swindled by experience—smoking at a pay-phone.
  I facetiously named him "Death in Venice":
I'd read Mann as tourist's homework. Our pre-boarding hours
  He spent passionately on the phone—to whom?
When a second phone at our gate rang, he stared at me
  As if I knew, within my sealed universe
Of coincidence, who was calling. The central fact,
  Simple, but difficult to put into words,
Was the note addressed to my traveling companion,
  Stefano Marchetti, on August 30th,
In Venice—a note waiting for him at the hotel
  When we arrived—and we immediately
Questioned how the correspondent knew to send the note
  Here to the Locanda Sturion, because
No friend of ours had this address, and this was no friend,
  But a stranger, Carlo, who'd misaddressed
His note: he'd written to a *Silvano* Marchetti,

Not to my Stefano. A coincidence?
Carlo called to repeat his plea that in an extreme
    Moment he needed shelter from great danger—
Would we permit him to spend the night on our bare floor?
    I felt this was the last crisis of a life
That had for years been drawing near to that precipice
    In secrecy and quiet, and now must claim
The loyalty of friends. Carlo could not understand
    That Stefano was not Silvano, that we
Knew nothing of their turbulent history, of errors
    Committed between them in the confusion
Of a foreign country. Stefano forbade Carlo
    A place by our side, but nothing explained how
Mysteriously Carlo had discovered the spot
    Where an approximation to his lost friend—
Nearly the same person, but a skewed portrait, misplaced
    Or damaged by rain—was passing through Venice
The night of the other's distress. I was visited
    by dreams of a weeping, faceless Silvano
Sought by Carlo through the universe; "Silvano" seemed
    A gap in the perfect world where a spirit
Heard the command to return to dust and disobeyed,
    Lingering a few minutes longer on earth
To ask of us, the living, a difficult favor—
    To hide him in our room, where his pursuer
Might neglect to look. If he could weather out the night
    He would tell us in the morning the answer
That blazed in that second when he heard his time was up.
    In the morning, a bald man with one black glove
Passed me in a square, and the next day, in Vicenza,
    He reappeared, Tarot-like, at our hotel
Where within the long arcade up Monte Berico
    I saw him stop to remove the glove and show
One false hand, like white chocolate, or soap. I've neglected
    To mention the most impressive augury—
Also the most conventional: in Venice we saw
    A coffin lowered into a gondola,
Mourners oared with the dead body down the dark canal—

The ultimate in picturesque, similar
To my foolish humming of the Hoffmann "Barcarolle"
    As we strolled by Rio dei Mendicanti . . .

In New York, a letter marked "hand-delivered" is taped
    To our door: Stefano's friend, Metro, has died—
His lingering cold which no one took seriously
    Wrapped him in a coma. Now he is ashes
Sprinkled in his backyard garden, planted just last spring.
    Metro died on the thirtieth of August,
The night we arrived in the city of gondolas,
    The night we received the enigmatic note
To Silvano: man telephoning in the airport,
    The one black glove, name I could call my terror.
Did Metro's soul, done with the body, come to Venice
    In the extreme moment? I've never written
An elegy: none of our small circle had yet died.
    This is not musical enough to sing his
Soul down the river mine and yours must, too, go down, but
    Metro needs a mourning song, not the white mask
We bought for him in Venice. We visited Keats' grave:
    The whole of Rome seemed to radiate around
Untimely death, a fact seen through a distractingly
    Beautiful circuit of tears. When I am dead
I may be wise enough to say it well. On the plane
    Back to New York I dreamed that Italian
Church facades also existed in America,
    But in our country they were not memorable:
I saw the intensity of a better epoch
    Drained from the columns—I could almost hold on
To pieces of the old distinction before I saw
    It fade into air. In San Gimignano
I felt a presentiment that I would spend next year
    Sanctifying my dreary premises: in court
My parents battle on my twenty-seventh birthday.
    I'm glad to age, greedy for each year I add
To my abacus, irrespective of sunderings
    That mar the date. Metro died at thirty-five,

A waste huge enough that I can address my parents
    Within the magic circle of his passing:
Let the fact of my body be the *Piramide*
    Memorial to your once marriage, and don't
Cry about things only seventy-five-percent sad—
    Save tears for the fully tragic. Metro's last
Fevered sentence was, "The answer is in the garden."
    I meet Metro in his still-tended garden
And I am wearing his clothes, given to me because
    We are one size. I want to read Metro's lips
For he is facing the invisible, and speaking
    Eloquently of efforts taken too late,
The many souls wandering in the air, not pinioned
    As children are. I am too corporeal
To hold the attention of one so weightless, to say,
    In a tone of sad confusion, that the good
Suit he wore in life fits me well, too well, like a charm.

■

Doctor Type

lives thirteen floors above and runs a practice
            in the basement. Off-duty he wears jeans
faded so white his butt "reads" (is discernible) across
the street before I recognize
            his face. I cry, "There's Doctor Type!"
in private

jubilation meant for no ear—but he hears.
            Does he understand I mean "archetype"?
I'm not accusing him of being a typist. I type,
and show the symptom of a man
            who types: shiftiness, a Gila
monster's dash

across a rock. I waived wood- and metalshop
                and took two years of typing: invert's choice.
Doctor Type is typical: he foreshadows. He's Jewish
or Arabic, *ca m'est egal.*
                I'm stuck on him. I have a crush.
His plump butt

signifies healing to me: his butt's the part
                from which I guess the Hippocratic whole.
Why don't I see him for a checkup? Premonitions
of embarrassing tumescence:
                Doctor Type's a family man
and would look

askance at the unsocial rising I'm prone
                to suffer when my dark epitome
shifts my testicles between his fingers to test for lumps.
Imagine telling Doctor Type
                this history of my body
"My flesh, lashed

by desire, couldn't help itself," I'd say,
                an idiot coquette, and Doctor Type
would warn, "Take care what you put in your mouth—make sure
it's sheathed." It blinds me to look back that far—
                to the embrace that will have been
the deadly

blow—the way one blast can burst the tympanum.
                My oral temperature's below normal
and I wake up sweating. I have two friends dead, one friend knows
he's dying. These words don't exist
                until I type them, and sometimes
type can't save

a thought from death: it clots, the way my blood
　　　　　froze as the messenger drove to the lab—
my blood turned to vermillion icicles, illegible.
I never gave a second tube.
　　　　　I spy, I shadow Doctor Type.
He nibbles

halvah between patients, and his practice swells;
　　　　　his wife is cooking couscous, Baby squalls.
Who wouldn't envy Doctor Type, or want his love? His butt
makes me wish to be born again—
　　　　　I'd be alert this time, sucking
in my gut

to pass more swiftly out. We'd chat—Mom, Doc, me—
　　　　　and he would snip my tiny foreskin off.
bad news blows like a sirocco through my nativity:
"It's not the Promised Land here, kid,"
　　　　　warns Doctor Type, and then he drops
the fishnet

in which I squirm. "You are free to go," he says,
　　　　　"if you can walk." The receptionist types
my bill, and saves—the cheapskate!—her nearly extinct carbon.
("You never know, there might be bits
　　　　　of useful ink left on this sheet.")
Doctor Type

shares the basement with a gay men's gym. My word
　　　　　for the hunks who lift weights there is *type:* "Cute
type!" I say when one struts past my window. Types are not drawn
to slight-physiqued non-types like me;
　　　　　types only flirt with other types.
My body,

pale, attracts mosquitoes. The bite by my left
      nipple will be worse tonight: I predict
by dawn it will eclipse the swelling on my knee. Wounds shift
powers, degrees, intensities.
      The wound that aches at dusk, by dawn
will be gone.

■

STEVE KOWIT

Josephine's Garden

First thing in the morning
the phone rings. It's Mary
to tell me that Jack,
after two years with AIDS,
has finally died.
An hour later the ophthalmologist
puts some sort of drops in my eyes
& for the rest of the day the light is blinding.
When I go outside I have to wear
those dark paper shades the nurse gave me—
even the pulpy grey stones
& the faded hedge & the pale
green spikes of the barrel cactus
in Josephine's garden
are too bright to look at,
while her roses & bougainvillea
blaze out as if someone had suddenly
flung back the shutters—
as blinding as one of those
high-mountain blizzards,
but more gorgeous
& painful.
If this is the way the world really is
it's too much to look at.
No one could ever survive it.
Nevertheless, all afternoon,
I keep stepping out into that garden,
eyes smarting as if someone
had rinsed them in acid. Astonished
again at the unbelievable colors.
The utter profusion of forms.
The sharp edges everything has in this world.

■

MICHAEL LASSELL

How to Watch Your Brother Die

When the call comes, be calm.
Say to your wife, "My brother is dying. I have to fly
to California."
Try not to be shocked that he already looks like
a cadaver.
Say to the young man sitting by your brother's side,
"I'm his brother."
Try not to be shocked when the young man says,
"I'm his lover. Thanks for coming."

Listen to the doctor with a steel face on.
Sign the necessary forms.
Tell the doctor you will take care of everything.
Wonder why doctors are so remote.

Watch the lover's eyes as they stare into
your brother's eyes as they stare into
space.
Wonder what they see there.
Remember the time he was jealous and
opened your eyebrow with a sharp stick.
Forgive him out loud
even if he can't understand you.
Realize the scar will be
all that's left of him.

Over coffee in the hospital cafeteria
say to the lover, "You're an extremely good-looking
young man."
Hear him say,

"I never thought I was good enough looking to
deserve your brother."
Watch the tears well up in his eyes. Say,
"I'm sorry. I don't know what it means to be
the lover of another man."
Hear him say,
"It's just like a wife, only the commitment is
deeper because the odds against you are so much
greater."
Say nothing, but
take his hand like a brother's.

Drive to Mexico for unproven drugs that might
help him live longer.
Explain what they are to the border guard.
Fill with rage when he informs you,
"You can't bring those across."
Begin to grow loud.
Feel the lover's hand on your arm,
restraining you. See in the guard's eye
how much a man can hate another man.
Say to the lover, "How can you stand it?"
Hear him say, "You get used to it."
Think of one of your children getting used to
another man's hatred.

Call your wife on the telephone. Tell her,
"He hasn't much time.
I'll be home soon." Before you hang up say,
"How could anyone's commitment be deeper than
a husband and wife?" Hear her say,
"Please, I don't want to know all the details."

When he slips into an irrevocable coma
hold his lover in your arms while he sobs,
no longer strong. Wonder how much longer

you will be able to be strong.
Feel how it feels to hold a man in your arms
whose arms are used to holding men.
Offer God anything to bring your brother back.
Know you have nothing God could possibly want.
Curse God, but do not
abandon Him.

Stare at the face of the funeral director
when he tells you he will not
embalm the body for fear of
contamination. Let him see in your eyes
how much a man can hate another man.

Stand beside a casket covered in flowers,
white flowers. Say,
"Thank you for coming" to each of several hundred men
who file past in tears, some of them
holding hands. Know that your brother's life
was not what you imagined. Overhear two mourners say,
"I wonder who'll be next."

Arrange to take an early flight home.
His lover will drive you to the airport.
When your flight is announced say,
awkwardly, "If I can do anything, please
let me know." Do not flinch when he says,
"Forgive yourself for not wanting to know him
after he told you. He did."
Stop and let it soak in. Say,
"He forgave me, or he knew himself?"
"Both," the lover will say, not knowing what else
to do. Hold him like a brother while he
kisses you on the cheek. Think that
you haven't been kissed by a man since
your father died. Think,

"This is no moment not to be strong." Fly
first class and drink scotch. Stroke
your split eyebrow with a finger
and think of your brother alive. Smile
at the memory and think
how your children will feel in your arms,
warm and friendly and without challenge.

■

PHILLIS LEVIN

What the Intern Saw

I

He saw a face swollen beyond ugliness
Of one who just a year ago
Was Adonis
Practicing routines of rapture:

A boy who could appear
To dodge the touch of time,
Immortal or immune—
A patient in a gown,
Almost gone.

II

In the beautiful school of medicine
He read about human suffering,
A long horrible drama
Until the screen of anaesthesia
And penicillin's manna.

But now, in myriad sheets
Of storefront glass refracting evening's
Razor blue, in a land of the freely
Estranged from the dead, he meets
That face and fear seizes his body.

III

His feet have carried him to bed.
He thinks he must be getting old
To so revise
His nature and his plan.

He shuts his eyes
And in his sleep he sees a gleaming bar,
The shore of pain.
It isn't far.
People live there.

■

ROBERT LOUTHAN

Syndrome

When we're done with this embrace,
which is final and encumbered with the gun
I've brought to bed because our loving was diseased
and you're dazzled now daily by pain,

when I lift my leg off your emaciated waist,
which I promise not to do before you're no longer living
and I'm no longer living to the beat of your heart,
when I've blasted the spot that I'm kissing on your temple,

go up and tell God I want you rocked in his lap,
and when he does it fuck his brains out.

■

The Brothers Grief

Men in Opera
still weep
on each other

's breast.
The brother
on the street

has no breast
to weep on;
his stomach empty

as he walks
until he has
to sleep

then he lies down
and sleeps where
the quiet dark is.

. . .   .

Weep not,
Brother,
Our brother is

dying of AIDS,
or cancer and he has
"passed on," expired.

"Do you believe in
Reincarnation" I
replied, "Which ones"

The brother on
the street or
the blind mother

in Florida, Brandon,
to be exact.
Precisely that

Oppen might say
if he were able
to speak clearly

from his rest home.

. . .   .

We've become
a nation of
Grieving Men.

And we say our silent prayers
as the Death of
Tennessee Williams is announced . . .

Or Martin Luther King,
or George Moscone,
or Harvey Milk . . .

Whoever the latest
Death-lists list.
We've grown up

With a large public
knowledge and
private sophistication.

Dali and Lorca,
Strange Political Bedfellows,
Indeed!!! The amount

of private lusts
shared between them
will never be known.

. . .   .

A public Dirgist
to find trust
in the men we love

and loved, trans
migrating . . ."And
the art," Auden said

"Are the only way
we have of breaking
bread with the dead."

Read that: bred
with the dead
as we assume

their spirit in
our passing
the fleshy corners

of our body politic.

■

RICHARD McCANN

Summer at the Jardin d'Hiver

We paid six francs to see *Droseraceae,* dead flies
touched to spiny lips, gluey tendrils waving
unstuck wings. The rest was dead, or waiting
like the Joshua tree, one cell holding water
until rain. Outside, all hung in the hour
before harvest. Inside, we inspected the dormant
rows, then crossed a bridge transecting the emptied
shallows of a man-made tropical lagoon.
Why had we come back here?
Another time we would have broken
windows to let in air and coax
all upwards; in winter
this would be the new heart, light flaming
through leaded greenhouse glass toward delicate
flowers opening. Beauty is never enough
expressed, nor does it spare us, yet what
inside of us demanded something other
than a glass dome over
extravagant forced blooms?

■

J . D . McCLATCHY

The Landing

Through the blinds, it must have been the streetlamp I saw
That silvered the woodwork. Step by step, its shadow was

Measuring out tonight. The climb itself has become a cloud
That thickens with the effort. I'd look up if I could.

Three lines erased in the address book. The thumbed pages
Of those last weeks through which the halflit end still gapes

Unwritten. And what I miss goes without saying. Has
The explanation even there been brief as a flame and its ash?

I speak to the air that takes these things finally as its own
Tell me who that is beyond the stairwell's next turning now.

■

Fog

A sheet of water turned over.
Sedge script. River erasure.
The smoke out of the factory
Stacks drifts to the title page—
Words too big to read, too quickly
Gone to say what they are.
The water machine is stalled
And sighs. There go last night's
Now forgotten dreams, airborne,
Homebound, on their way to work.

*

Again this morning: five-storey elm spoons
Stirring the wheylight, fur on the knobby
Melon rind left in the sink, the china egg
Under the laying hen, the quilt's missing
Patch, and now the full moon's steamed-up
Shaving mirror leaning against the blue.

*

When my daughter died, from the bottom
Of every pleasure something bitter
Rose up, a sour taste of nausea,
The certain sense of having failed
Not to save her but in the end to know
I could not keep her from passing
As through the last, faintest intake
Of breath to somewhere unsure of itself,
The dim landscape that grief supposes.
I remember how, in the hospital,
Without a word she put her glasses on
And stared ahead, just before she died.

I take mine off these days, to see
More of my solitude, its incidental
Humiliations. Nothing satisfies
Its demand that she appear in order
To leave my life over and over again.
If, from my car, I should glimpse her
In a doorway, bright against the dark
Inside, and stop and squint at the glare—
It's a rag on a barbed-wire fence.
Or I spot her in a sidewalk crowd
But almost at once she disappears
The way one day slips behind the next.
I've come to think of her now, in fact,
Or of her ghost I guess you'd have to say,
As the tear that rides and overrides
My eye, so that the edges of things go
Soft, a girl is there and not there.

*

Even in the dark
The long shadow of the stars
Drifts beneath the pines.

*

Snagged on a stalk: fresh tufts of rabbit down,
Thistle silk, a thumbnail's lot of spittle spawn.

*

Fidgeting among the goateed professors
And parlor radicals at the *Pension Russe,*
The girls whispered to themselves
About the tubercular young Reinhard,
Alone at a corner table, smoking,
Who had introduced them to immortality
By burning a cigarette paper
And as the ash plummeted upward
Exclaiming *"Die Seele fliegt!"*

*

It's the first breath of the dead
That rises from the firing squad
While the anarchist who squealed
Gets drunk and argues with God.

It's Shelley's lung in the lake
And his hand in the ashes on shore.
It's the finespun shirt he ordered
And the winding sheet he wore.

*

When the two famous novelists discovered
Each the other in the same dress—
A shot-silk "creation" or orris-dust
Laid on blanched silver, like the irony
That is the conscience of style, obscuring
To clarify, bickering to be forgiven—
One retired with her pale young admirers,
Disdain for whom creamed up in her tea,
To a folly by the buckled apple tree.
She sat and pretended to listen to herself
Being praised, picking at grizzled lichen
On the bench, like drops of blistered enamel.

The other tugged at her pearls and stayed
Near the smiles, her dress insinuated
Among the lead crystal teardrops
On the chandelier above her, each one
The size, and now the color, of a blossom
On an apple bough outside, and herself
Inside, tiny and helplessly upside-down.

*

The first month of the first marriage.
The second year of the second marriage.
The third betrayal of the third marriage.
And love. Love. Always love.

*

a deep winter yawn

        the wind caught drowsing

static on the news

        charred ozone glaze

dead-petal weather

        the air's loose skin

the albino's birthmark
>> the vinegar mother
a bubble in the artery
>> the pebble in Demosthenes' mouth
love asleep at the wheel
>> childhood stunned and dumped
the philosopher's divorce
>> the psychopomp's coin
self-pity's last tissue
>> the blister on the burn
the emptiness added daily
>> the abstract's hive
quarry of doubts
>> earthrise from the dark side
the holy sleeve
>> the beatific blindness
white root of heaven
>> the hedge around happiness

*

The sound of it? A silence
Understood as all the noise
Ignored or stifled, nods
Exchanged on the trading floor,
Or sex in the next room,
His hand over her mouth,
her belt, the overcast leather,
Clenched between his teeth.

Where the needle stuck,
Its hiss and hard swallow
Halfway into the heart
Of the nocturne, two notes
Fell further apart, the space
Between them a darkness

Clotting, the moon
Having passed behind
A black key, then risen
Higher across the record's
Rutted, familiar road.

*

Suddenly, lengths of storm gauze
Drawn across the clearing.
We must not want too much
To know. Uncertainty
Condenses on the windshield
Then runs down the cheek,
A single waxen tear.
When last night's grief
Is pulled back from,
Who will be the brighter?
Hush. Be careful. Turn
Those headlights down, low
As a curtained candle flame
Shivering in the dark dispelled.

*

First, the diagnosis: those night sweats
And thrush, the breathing that misplaces air,
The clouds gathering on a horizon of lung . . .
Translated as *pneumocystis,* the word from a dead
Language meant to sound like a swab
On a wound open but everywhere unseen.
Then, the options. There were options,
Left like food trays outside your door.
Protocols, support groups, diets,
A promising treatment.

But three months later
You began to forget the doctor's appointments,
And the next week no longer cared that you forgot.
The friends who failed to visit, even their letters
Grew hard to parse. It was not as if their "real"
Feelings lay between the lines, but that the lines
Themselves would break apart: *the fight so long*
All your work   the circumstances   remember when.
But remember was precisely what you couldn't do,
And to pay attention more than you could afford.
The books you'd read now looked back at you
With blank pages memories might fill in
With makeshift, events haphazardly recalled—
Snow swarming on the canal that Christmas
In Venice with Claudio who cried to see it,
Or globes of watery sunlight in your Chelsea flat,
White lilacs at their lips last May, no one there
For a change but just you two.
                                        And here you are
Still, propped up in the halflight, my shadow,
My likeness, your hand wandering to the arm
Of the chair, as if your fingers might trace
The chalkdust of whole years erased.
Is this, then, what it means to lose your life?
But the question is forgotten before it can be
Answered. I take your hand, and give it back
To you, and watch you then look up, giving in,
Unknowing all, whose pain has just begun.

■

HEATHER McHUGH

What Hell Is

March 1985

Your father sits inside
his spacious kitchen, corpulent
and powerless. Nobody knows
how your disease is spread; it came
from love, or some
such place. Your father's bought
with forty years of fast talk, door-to-door,
this fancy house you've come home now to die in.
Let me tell you what
hell is, he says: I got this
double fridge all full of food
and I can't let my son go in.

*

Your parents' friends
stop visiting. You are a damper on
their spirits. Every day you feel
more cold (no human being
here can bear
the thought—it's growing
huge, as you grow thin).
Ain't it a bitch, you say, this
getting old? (I'm not sure
I should laugh. No human being
helps, except
suddenly, simply
Jesus: him you hold.)

*

We're not allowed
to touch you if you weep or bleed.
Applying salve to sores that cannot heal
your brother wears a rubber glove.
With equal meaning, cold or kiss
could kill you. Now what do I mean
by love?

*

The man who used
to love his looks
is sunk in bone
and looking out.

Framed by immunities
of telephone and lamp
his mouth is shut,
his eyes are dark.

While we discuss despair
he is it, somewhere
in the house. Increasingly
he's spoken of

not with. In kitchen
conference we come
to terms that we
can bear. But where is he?

In hell, which is
the living room.
In hell, which has
an easy chair.

■

By Faith Not Sight

We cannot get
out of ourselves
to be sure
no atom feels, no

heaven comprehends and so
we simply hope.
Our senses (five
or six) describe

ourselves. (Could being be
so numbered?) All the little
strata of the world—the
audible and visible

of frequencies, the
findable and thinkable
of facts—could they
be fashioned

by and for our expert self-
importances? Somebody
I adored has died

into unbearability.
But where is that?
Is where a narrow
inquiry? We aren't

our lives, or anything we made
in man or camera's image—where
is where itself? Who's
who? The issue's not

rhetorical: exactly what
we most require
we're most required
to give. And even love

(especially love)
became a homelessness.
Now that he's dead
where can I live?

■

Third Person Neuter

Is God mad? Was Christ
crazy? Is the truth
the legal truth? (Three PhD's who swear

the human being who believes
a human being God
is what, in fairness, speaking

clinically, we call
a nut.) No jury,
given sacred laws

of science and democracy, would now
forgive so big a claim as Christ's—a claim
for good. (The wounded get

their settlements in millions, not
worlds-without-end.) We think of bliss
as ignorance, and heaven as naivete: the doctor's

a philosopher, the priest a practicing
apologist. Not one of them
will let me see

with my own eyes my friend again.
When experts gave him time, it made
his luck and language die. What good

was love? It was the ultimate
authority to quit.
He had no use

for flesh at last
and, Christ,
I'm made of it.

■

J A M E S   M E R R I L L

T w o   P o e m s   f o r
D a v i d   K a l s t o n e

1. Investiture at Cecconi's

Caro, that dream (after the diagnosis)
found me losing patience outside the door of
"our" Venetian tailor. I wanted evening
clothes for the new year.

Then a bulb went on. The old woman, she who
stitches dawn to dusk in his back room, opened
one suspicious inch, all the while exclaiming
over the late hour—

Fabrics? patterns? those the proprietor must
show by day, not now—till a lightning insight
cracks her face wide: *Ma! the Signore's here to
try on his new robe!*

Robe? She nods me onward. The mirror triptych
summons three bent crones she diffracted into
back from no known space. They converge by magic,
arms full of moonlight.

Up on my own arms glistening sleeves are drawn. Cool
silk in grave, white folds—Oriental mourning—
sheathes me, throat to ankles. I turn to face her,
uncomprehending.

Thank your friend, she cackles, *the Professore!*
Wonderstruck I sway, like a tree of tears. You—
miles away, sick, fearful—have yet arranged this
heartstopping present.

2. Farewell Performance

Art. It cures affliction. As lights go down and
Maestro lifts his wand, the unfailing sea change
starts within us. Limber alembics once more
make of the common

lot a pure, brief gold. At the end our bravos
call them back, sweat-soldered and leotarded,
back, again back—anything not to face the
fact that it's over.

You are gone. You'd caught like a cold their airy
lust for essence. Now, in the furnace parched to
ten or twelve light handfuls, a mortal gravel
sifted through fingers,

coarse yet grayly glimmering sublimate of
palace days, Strauss, Sidney, the lover's plaintive
Can't we just be friends? which your breakfast phone call
clothed in amusement,

this is what we paddled a neighbor's dinghy
out to scatter—Peter who grasped the buoy,
I who held the box underwater, freeing
all it contained. Past

sunny, fluent soundings that gruel of selfhood
taking manlike shape for one last jete on
ghostly—wait, ah!—point into darkness vanished.
High up, a gull's wings

clapped. The house lights (always supposing, caro,
Earth remains your house) at their brightest set the
scene for good: true colors, the sun-warm hand to
cover my wet one. . . .

Back they come. How you would have loved it. We in
turn have risen. Pity and terror done with,
programs furled, lips parted, we jostle forward
eager to hail them,

more, to join the troupe—will a friend enroll us
one fine day? Strange, though. For up close their magic
self-destructs. Pale, dripping, with downcast eyes they've
seen where it led you.

■

Your   Sightless   Days

Blind eyes could blaze like meteors and be gay
Dylan Thomas

I remember clearly deciding not to see
anymore myself this out of sheer protest
or only see what I could tell you the whole of
art was out so was anything new the near
buff hillside gone to grass was just our speed
but of course I was always minimizing
as if to say there's nothing to see today
it's the same old thing Rog sycamore's bare
park full of Seurats but hey feel that breeze
and knowing how clear Aegean blue your eyes were
please I know what I watched go out but even
when it struck us down blacked our windows
like an air raid even then your glimmering half
sight was so seductive *What do you see*
I'd ask you coaxing every street sign like
they were glyphs off a ruined temple night
would fall you'd frown *Are the lights on Paul*
and tear my heart all the Bette Davis lines
out to get us but oh my dearest every one
was on spots flashes searches long white tubes
like the swords in *Star Wars* candlepower fit
for a Byzantine saint and still so dim the dark
so jealous of life and then out of nowhere
a neon day of LA sun we're out strolling
you stop peer impish intent as a hawk
and say *I see you* just like that and THEN
I toss my blinders and drink the world like water
till the next dark up and down for half a year
the left one gone in April overnight

two millimeters on the right side saved
and we fought for those that knife of light
and beaten ground raging for day like the
Warsaw ghetto all summer long I dripped
your veins at 4 and midnight watching every
drop as if it was sight itself so did we
win did we lose you died with the barest
shadows oh I know but even then we hoped
a cataract laser might give us a glint
would not see night as the way of the world
and what have I seen since your blindness my
love just that my love requires no eyes so
why am I tapping this thin white cane of outrage
through crowds of sighted fools the pointless trees
and the awful dusk unlifting some few colors
bright as razor blades trying to make me look
I'm shut tight Oedipus-old leave me alone
I have somehow gotten it all wrong because
when you were the blackest blind you laughed *laughed*
groped your way and stared the noon sun down
How are you jerks would ask *Read Job* you'd say
a gleam in every good hour pulling out puns
and Benny jokes and fighting to read the charts
knowing the worst had fallen you'd hoot on the phone
and wrestle the dog so the summer was still
the summer Rog see how you saw us through

■

B u c k l e y

favors castration or failing that a small
tattoo on the upper thigh in the thick-haired
swirl by the balls hot and rank in a Bike
no shower hockeysweat Buckley's upper
lip fairly puckers at the thought or else
a scarlet letter F I guess but cubist

Buckley's in no rush he's breaking bread with
Lady Couldn't-You-Di and sailing to
Byzantium for the weekend moonless nights
he lies on deck and dictaphones the tale
of Bucko Bill countercounterspy and Company
ubermensch Turnbull and Assered to the tits
stoically libidinous if pressed
at tennis a prince and vingt-et-un how far
from the terminal wing the suites are asked
the doe-eyed cons in Sing Sing Buckley keeps
in cigs and Nestles pleading the dago guv
for Clemenceau the traitor every peace
is dirty pink triangles have a nice
retro feel & for quarantine there's islands
off Cape Ann so bare and stony no Brahmin'd
be caught dead on its lea shore a Statue of
Bondage blindfold torch snuffed a whole theme park
of hate monorail geek-dunk Inquisition
daily 10 and 3 heigh-ho mouse-eared dwarfs
in Future Perfect a mushroom cloud like spun
sugar oh Buckley the thing is I agree
about Soviet wheat the Shah the Joint Chiefs
can have all the toilet seats they like but
somehow your pantaloons are in a froth
to cheerlead the dying of my pink people
covered with a condom head to toe St. Paul
of the boneyard guillotining dicks bug-eyed
which reminds me who does the makeup on
Firing Line Frank E. Campbell how did you
get to be such a lady without surgery
I want my F for fag of course on the left
bicep twined with a Navy anchor deck
of Luckies curled in my tee sleeve just the look
to sport through a minefield beating a path
to smithereens arm in arm friend & friend
bivouacked 2 by 2 odd men out so
far out they can almost see over the wall
no more drilling Latin to meatbrain boys

not 50 before they're 30 not skittish
and not going back in Bill no matter how
many cardinals sit on your face oh rest
easy the spit on your grave will pool and mirror
the birdless sky and your children's children
kneel in the waste dump scum of you a popish
rot greening their knees and their Marcos earrings
and spring will maggot the clipped Connecticut
yard of your secret heart ink and bleed me
name and number and I will dance on you

■

Waiting   to   Die

takes longer now: whole pharmacies of pain
killers and stopgaps, arsenals of slow
motion hand grenades lobbed at the viral
castle. The trickier thing is where to wait:
you pay by the day, no weekly rates in peak
season. Some are wasted at home craning
out the last bedroom window, some in camps
barbed in the high Mojave, very Japanese
in feeling. Some have no idea where.
Nobody waits all day, not every minute,
there's always sleep. Just last August I stopped
in David's garden, heatstruck as a sundial,
woozy with memory overload, forgetting
the late hour. Van Gogh waited in San Remy
blissed out on a jailyard's flowers, alive
as long as the irises, not dying half
so much as they. Go with the first frost
if possible, miss nothing green. David's place
wide as an island breaks into dogwood,
cherry and wild crab in about ten weeks—

too late now. Whereas spring is already out
of its mind in California, foothills gripped
by sudden pasture, moss on clay, overnight
jasmine clear as a bell. Mid-February
is May here, these narrow weeks of Irish
and months and months of summer coming, pale
as straw and ready to burn. "I look like
E.T.," David drawled, fetching a friend to
supper, careless of shuddering *maitre d's,*
fingers drumming Gershwin. A medicine chest
rides us like a sidecar, like the red-nosed
Fields with his hip flask: *I always carry*
a bottle of snake-oil in my pocket. Carry
the snake too. Spring grows steeper and
steeper, its fifty million irises alone.
Still, there must be something in bloom
somewhere to set on the snow of David's winter
island, being as the roses missed him.
A southern boy learns to play hard to get
before he's out of short pants. So do we
flirt with death, every stem we cut, the riot
of life in a single flower that will not last
the weekend. He never saw Hawaii at all
or anywhere West of East. "Oh you'll love it,"
I raptured, thoughtless in my August swoon.
Once I saw a hardy Boston lady stroke
a pot of ivy above her sink. "Westminster
Abbey," she boasted, who'd smuggled a cutting
through Customs in her purse. Why not that?
A specimen slip from the far edge of aloha,
cliffs for miles vertical green, exploding
orchids down a rotted volcano, rimless
emerald. Its furthest valley is a box
canyon facing the sea, unapproachable
by land. They don't have spring in places
that have no reason. There the leper Koolau
made his stand, him and a band of others

as other as he, who would not go to Molokai
when the great roundup gathered the stooped
and limbless, locking them in waiting rooms.
Angry like us Koolau held his valley
twenty years, the knit of his skin intricate
as a spider tattoo. Something from there would be
nice and gaudy in David's room, whose windows
command the white secret of his garden. A jade
plum sweet as Carolina after rain, borne
ten thousand miles, Venus chasing Mars across
the starry sky. Whatever hurts, whatever
dies at home, bring in flowers as long as
you can, because you are going West
where David is too soon, under this island,
all your waiting done. So go in bloom.

David Almgren
2.14.88
West Island

■

Ed Dying

Hate is an old man fucking, arduous
and half a bone, but I work at it
like Sophie Tucker, a last geriatric fling
like pushing a car uphill with a rope.
Hate the Reagans and their facile cancers,
all straight people with lives and my brothers
who flee to the continent having buried
their allotment. This is the rage of the 8th
year, bent out of shape, crazily displaced,
yelling at the queerest people because
the scum politicos of the NIH are out
of reach, funding the end of the world.

I massacre whoever gets in my small way—check
lost in the mail, promise of shirts Friday,
876-4466 my Thrifty druggist rings busy busy
and I need refills like a one-arm bandit,
that kind of thing. As for Ed, Ed is dying
by phone, dwindling in secret, doing without
spunk and visitors. I leave word weekly
on his machine, reports of my latest tantrum,
a recent self-immolation in the Mayfair checkout.
For months there is no reply, but we are
light-years beyond good manners, Ed and I,
loathing bullshit so and the comfort of sunny
disposition. Checked in the day Rita Hayworth died:
Hi Ed, poor Gilda, huh? My only friend who knows
how blonde the lady from Shanghai was and why
it matters so. Publicity errs on the bright side
always, burning for us to have a good time.
Ed who has met them all—Cary, Hitch, Her Serene
Highness—is the last living link between us
poor queens and *To Catch a Thief,* speaking of Eden
lost. Now we are all on the last train out,
fleeing fleeing, diamonds up our ass, the past
curling like smoke as Marlene drags her last
Gitane. Even as Ed is dying, in Washington
everyone eats his boogers and Mormons file
the plague under Pest Control, Reagan's colon
clear as a bagpipe, his sausage tumors
replicated in lifelike vinyl for souvenirs.
Then suddenly over New Year's: *This is Ed.*
Thank you for all your messages. I love
your rage. So I hate mostly for Ed's sake now,
and the old man fucking with his dick in a brace
has mounted a bimbo who can't feel it, does it
for fifty, next year will do it for thirty-five
and eat his shorts for an encore. There are easier
ways than all this slamming about, I admit,
but the time comes—say after the third pneumonia,

and they send you home to recuperate with
the wrong dose, 200 fucking milligrams less
than what will make you live again, and ten
days later you're back in stir, starting it all
over, over and over—the time will come
when you prove you are still alive just feeling
anything at all. So sometimes we are wronged
as Lana Turner in the fifties, jilted and stomped,
herded like misfits, the vanishing years aching
like a torrent of smoke thrown by a moonlit train
bound for the chaos of Shanghai. And if we wail
and spew bile we say we are not collaborators,
for Ed would not be dying please without
the complicity of niceness, so many smiling
colon exams. Yes it's hard to keep it up,
me and this numb member of mine, rutting
while Rome burns, but to hate everything
half-true—including me, especially me—
a nasty temper works like Spanish fly.
Be hard and cry foul, I order my bad thing,
for we are in enemy hands, buying time like
fallen women in countries torn by the death
grip of keeping things polite. Hate for the same
reason a man might sit and weep: missing Ed.

■

4 0

oh boy oh boy four years to go before
Robert Louis Stevenson dies in Samoa
gimme four more and I'll get a degree
in Greek statues I'll learn Chinese be kind
to my dearest enemies lady lady
save us a dance it's coming down in sheets

out there rivers of frangipani white
clouded peaks the cold volcanoes oh please
be kind to us who are not kidnapped save
by demons we father forth 40's half
a death these days World War I all over
the flower of a generation gone
to bits in Flanders like a rugby match
gone haywire all the poets gunned and buttered
till only Shaw was left to grow up and
Rebecca West grew barren as the wives
of ancient Thebes and life sucked no more tea
look the UN is 40 and solves nothing
and I saw day ten weeks after the light
show at Hiroshima and also solved
nothing ask any phobic it's not the heights
it's the edges that get you that weird thing
of being drawn to the precipice do it
the time has come to take the plunge and none
of your youthly coy and basket shots will
save you time doesn't give a fuck oh but
we planned such plans if the war hadn't come
and the weather had held and life had cleared
like a late Manet the scot died half a world
from the cinder choke of his native damp
and so will I bone-thin and sunburned blown
like a sailor take my slot in the coral
chambers still if I must be me not him
no buccaneer silver Jekyll and Hyde
to make me fit for a boy to read if I
must go early give me please one friend one
year but nothing's enough and the cliffs at Thera
where the old world ended tomorrow my love
is a stolen kiss but we sail together
if we sail at all hey 40's kid stuff

■

To GB from Tuscany

Always wondering what's left besides us
and how much time, I stare at the bright
fall of morning on the gray/blue columns
of Santo Spirito, the calm stone of Brunelleschi
washed smooth in a river of mind over matter.
Galileo believed in the opposite of God
for which the penalty was being shut up
with the truth, like cellmates. There is no
gay life in Italy, they all want to go
to New York, not having heard it is
no longer there. I can't tell you how much
you would like today, the pomegranates
heaped in baskets, air drowsy with wood-smoke,
last night a wind down the Arno that set
the moon's teeth on edge. In 1348 the Plague
took a third of Florence, four out of five
in Siena, and there were no baths to close.
Now and then you will see soldiers with nothing
to fight, eating gelato around a Jeep,
and one will look like he just posed
for Michelangelo, who sculpted what he could
not have or be. Or even more naked still,
the courtiers in striped tights and codpieces
strutting in the Piccolomini frescoes, as if
they didn't inhabit an age of blood
that ate young men for breakfast. You'd like
the burnt-siena of the cleared fields,
the pang of yellow shivering through the vines,
scholarly rows of sycamores leading you down
a country road with a promise that nothing ends.
I am not a fan of autumn even so,
but would like to split with you a Tuscan apple
half and half. The light is so clear at four
that every cypress stiffens, honey seeps

in every crevice, no wall escapes the gold
flaunting like a slut. What we seek
from love is depth of field, precisely what
we go to countries for. I brought no camera
on this trip, can no more freeze in time
the rosy stone of Assisi than I can
our numbers. Which of the painters of the 1300s
(who can keep them straight) got left behind
in '48? Next time I promise we'll go
together. But I warn you, my friend: in Italy
the men of our tribe live with their widowed
mothers, and the mothers never die. A perfect
circle, that. Monday a black-eyed monk, say 30,
cruised me for half a second in the nave
not 50 feet from where Saint Francis
lies still as a bird with no way south.
Where we are going otherwise I cannot say
beyond November, but these are the shades of marble
a Tuscan hill is capable of: cobalt, ash,
midnight, green ink, tawny, blinding white,
stones fit for a jeweler, towers of them,
streets cobbled with vulcan rock that gleams
like jet in the rain. I miss you of course,
but you know that part. The queer thing is,
Tuscany has already started to be
a dream again, even to me. The last night
I sit at the mouth of the Tiber, on a harbor
shaded by plane trees, eating calamari
fried, and don't know what I am bringing home.
You can have half of whatever it is, once
I change my *lire* back to dollars. Think of
the apple as down payment. In certain
Tuscan places you begin to see how time,
like anything else worth the covering
of autumn ground—us for instance—mines
its gold and shimmer from the deepest field,
even when the days grow short. Such light.

■

H O N O R   M O O R E

M e m o i r

For J. J. Mitchell,
dead of AIDS 7/26/86

I first remember you in Paris, blaze
of a smile, eleven years ago. Today
Joan tells me you're dead, the first I've loved
dead of that disease. It was New Year's Eve.
We sat on St. Germain drinking, watching
a boy in a black and white, convict-striped
Edwardian bathing suit weave festive
traffic on a skateboard—you, wild with
talk and blond hair. We had run into you
and Joe, and with you we walked to a dark
turreted flat on Ile St. Louis to meet
the silent, pale boy who was your lover.

I would not have said love then, didn't know
as we drank I watched your face to learn
what ignited your laugh: How might I live
to come to that? You lived outside Paris,
"in a forest" you said, at an old mill
with a famous woman painter. My mother
had died. The man I loved bored me. You had
drugs and you were homosexual. I
wouldn't have said I too had drugs, was
in my wine where you were in whatever
one drinks with a famous woman at the end
of her looks, or smokes with a quiet boy.

"He killed himself," you said, smoking on the street
years later in New York. I didn't say
I had become homosexual, and you
didn't say the boy's death had caused you much
aside from anger. But you got sober. Paul
said so Christmas Eve before he left us
to cook what he would serve at your bed.
And I got sober. Today when Joan
told me of your death, we both said, "but he was
in recovery." The young woman who
drank with you amazed at a boy on a skate
New Year's Eve never saw you grin sober,

but I have the image of Paul and St. Marks
days after your death, waving. I didn't
know what I was learning in how he lifted
his hand, but I have what the loss meant:
how his hat hid his eyes, how blond winter
grass hides a blue pond as I stop my car now
to speak a prayer for the dead. "Sober you can
do anything," you told Joan. Jimmy said
your last days the virus at your brain had you
in summer at the door on Fire Island
offering refreshment as guests arrived,
beautiful men, one after another.

■

CAROL MUSKE

The Eulogy

The man in the black suit delivers a eulogy
each page he turns, turns
a page of light on the ceiling,

because if death mimics us, mocking
the eye's cowardly flight
from the flower-covered coffin

to the framed photo of the bereaved, alive.
It is not night.
It is California.

There are hibiscus dropping
their veined shrouds
on the crushed-stone path outside.

A gold cufflink blazes
as the eulogist raises his hands.

Shadows alter the ceiling,
the readable text.
There are two ways to meet death,

he says. One fearful,
the other courageous.
One day purposeful, the next hopeless.

One young man died because he had sex.
The eulogist speaks of soldiers under fire,
the cowards and the heroes.

A woman next to me cannot stop
weeping. I can find no tears inside
me. The cufflinks beam

signals at us, above us.
The sun through the skylight
grows brighter and brighter:

Watch now, God,
Watch the eulogist raise his hands.
The rays, like your lasers,

blind the front rows.
The gifts love gives us!
Some of us flinch, some do not.

■

A p p l a u s e *

for Paul Monette

1

Not the glittering shudder in the ear, the high whine of the wasp,
Not the drunk holding up a glass, getting eloquent; nor
percussive, furious, the steady drum on the desk of the child

who doesn't get it. Not the echoing blow to the right temple
of the guard patrolling the green lawns of the industrial giant,
the hail of stones and beercans onstage at the rock concert—

nor the thunk-thunk of a pistol whipping,
the eerie scree of someone screwing gun to silencer.
Applause has no opposite, contains its own poles—
yet it might be said that the soundlessness of the newly dead,

* Title of a photograph exhibit by Holly Wright

the preternaturally-silent chorus of, in this news photograph,
a family, drowned on their way here from Haiti is audible.
still afloat, lashed to their tiny illegal raft—hands folded
together, like this, like applause for the end, the soul's tortured bow
     and exit.

2

Applause has a place: punctual comment,
forever hearing itself, even in a mob. As if clapping
is thought, a glass hatch high above everything, but
occasionally caught off-guard—like the woman or man
who moves air traffic across the skies, psyching out
the 3-D screen, piping the scoop in the earphones direct
to the pilots. Those steady voice blips, split suddenly with deific
     chitter,

surprise! God is a space chimp, communicating
from his little phobic cell circling earth, razzing the planets.
Intercepting the perfunctory hand-off, airport to port,
the altitude drift—God the screecher, God the stomper,
God the whistler in the balcony: they listen to twisting static,
hungry for his holy voice, his Bronx cheers. God in his tiny
monkey space-suit, chewing up the tubes of all the technology
he never mastered, God the Glitch, clapping his ugly furry little
     mitts.

3

You're clapping. In the photo for Holly's exhibit,
One shot of each subject, face and hands, maybe thirty in all,
each photo on the wall of a circular room and the people
photographed are applauding. If you stand in the center
of that room, they applaud *you.*
                    Nice conceit. Nice comment
on perspective. Nice immediate drift toward the philosophical.
Like Goya, the pure strain on the image can bend to political
     argument.

182

See that fat man clapping? He's mean, he doesn't want to do it,
but others are, so he tries to make his rhythm revisionist, one half
    second off.
See the other guy, preoccupied, going over his bills in his head
as he claps? Or the woman in the flowered hat, thrilled
to be an audience, thrilled to be a pair of long black theatre gloves,
    one thrilled glass eye?

4

Straight into the eyes of you, a real close-up,
making those palms applauding an unnatural act—
but so what? you seem to say. Your gaze labors to be direct:
too aware of the ironies of the so-called candid shot.
You look like a theatre-goer, lit by the shifting prism
of stagelight. Ladies, gentlemen, the audience takes
its seat in familiar anonymity, but wait—
your hands keep meeting in mid-air.
You don't stop clapping, even after the others do.
That's who she photographed, seventh row, no heckler,
but you in that instant you don't stop, you go on
applauding every moment, though I know that's my projection.
Because your friend is in the photograph next to you—
still alive then, so joyous, I don't think I've ever seen a man look
    that happy.

5

I suppose it happened something like this.
A woman got up (because the moon was full, because
her newborn was going to live now, after all, because
the fire of dung and grass did not, for once, go out)—
and began to dance. She moved her hips inside the animal skin,
the firelight made her look so huge that he loved her
and wanted just to see her there attached to her great shadow.
Seeing her shuffle and hop, he started to make a sound
with his hands. She looked up. It was not the slap of bare feet

on stone, not the bones of the dead in the wind, but a bearded
ugly appreciator she would come to call by name. He was saying
with his hands: I am looking at you and you are my delight
and this sound makes clear who I am. I am the one watching
you and saying it is good, making my two hands the collision of
    love and power.

6

Grape laboring over grape out of dark green leafage,
out of the woven balsa strips of the scuppernong, set
against the white stucco wall of the garage, set off-kilter
like a leaf-crown sliding over the eye of Bacchus. Years later,
in Perugia, in the blue valley at wine-harvest, I found
the sweet life-source of it, the image, the bare-bottomed
children in the mother's arms, the vats of grape, the hand-clap
at dusk in the cobbled street: *come home.* The day of his funeral,
your friend, I noticed the arbor near the Chapel of Memory,
rife with pale blue-green grapes against the white tiles. I
didn't think of wine, or new-minted money—I thought of
a shift downward from thought as they brought the coffin past,
a cliché of hearing: waves, cicadas, or the wind's slow applause
through the graveyard trees—it was just that sound seemed so
necessary—a dog barking, a plane—something of this life to
    salute him, anything.

7

Well, what did we expect? You and I
were joking once that the self is a path
of stepping-stones sinking in the black water:
now the self is nothing more than a sound.
Like the dawn rain, *om,* anahat, 4th Chakra,
the sound of two things *not* hitting
together. Annie draws faces in the air with her finger,
expects us to see who and where they are, say
excuse me when we walk through them. *Excuse me,*

I'm walking through my ex-lovers, my mother and father,
I'm walking through Jesus and Coco Chanel, Torquemada
and Simone Weil, poets living and dead, *excuse me*—
sound waves of one person standing up,
clapping the whole time, not for an encore, but for the end,
    the end of it.

8

In irresistible eclipse, two shadow jets converge
on the cypher-green screen: the controller spills
his coffee, screaming into the mouthpiece of the headset.
Gets drifting static, the wind, night, fog. He
doesn't see the sky light up once, twice, two hundred
miles south but he sways in place and calls them to him:
pilot, flight attendants, the woman in the fifteenth row
nursing her infant, the toddler racing up and down the aisles
(stopped forever mid-stride), the elderly vacationers,
the whole living matrix, sitting tight in a horseshoe,
flung out there beyond direction. Huddled like an audience,
or the gallery of people pictured applauding, while
the dark figure in the spotlight beckons—they stay so animated,
so still, refusing to imagine it: the act of relinquishing *thought*
then joining whatever it is in that huge specific light onstage.

9

Walked in to polite applause. (The teacher-keepers
had insisted: *be nice or else.*) Thirty-six or so
teenage mothers, runaways, j.d.'s, misfits, abused
babies. They looked, at first, like one big leer:
Impress us, poet-ess. God, should I read Plath?
Then it came back to me: the raw gleam of those nights
at Riker's. Poems of the oil spill, the ruptured tanker
roiling on the top-water, sullen ink on the inmates' fingers,
Then a torch hits the slick: flames
skyscraper-high. These brows furrow the same,

they write their Letters to God, Mamma or an Unborn
Child. Here's a hurt girl, head down, reading hers—
from a dead kid. "Don't do what my mamma did
to me, with drugs": —*I was like a butterfly wrapped
in a cocoon. She cut my wings, then my eyes, she took
my five senses, she wove that white powder into my shroud.*

10

It was After Care, the name of the program,
some obscure branch of New York City services.
Our job: to find jobs for "ex-offenders," newly-ex.
A simple task? For a twenty-four-year-old
student of Marcuse, enemy of the state: Piece of cake.
Fast talk. I called up Chase Manhattan—
You mean you *don't* want to hire a first-class
booster, to work the vault? Or Ma Bell:
She's good with numbers I said of the hooker in front
of me. Ma said no, so did the hooker. Why should
she scrape for ninety bucks a week when a good night
brought six hundred? *Dumb flatback!* She sneered,
clapped when a friend said she wanted to go straight.
"You sittin' on your money-maker!" I heard that quote over
and over that hot hot summer, on the phone, sweating,
I sat flat on my money-maker, using my big money-loser
to re-think economic politics. But then, I've always been
surprised to find the world just the way the cynics made it.

11

What happens to that youthful formality of purpose?
(I feel like I'm lost, do you? Listening to everyone
applauding a play I missed.) Spring here in L.A. today,
ninety or so, everything in bloom. I drive my four-
year-old to pre-school and turn off Santa Monica
into a stakeout. Top-lit cop cars jackknifed onto lawns,

a chopper churning the smog, an amplified voice:
Give up while you can. Come out with your hands raised.
My kid doesn't look up from her book, *The Big Orange Splot.*
All the hyper-tense police phrasing doesn't phase her.
I stare at a woman on the curb, solemnly applauding
the police—as if this is a film set. Perhaps it is.
But who's in that house? Finally, we're allowed to pass,
the choppers hand and sway. *Who was in that house?*
I woke, wondering, today, and who's in my life in this aftershock
    of shock, L.A.?

12

Each day's lack of point is why we lower ourselves
between armrests in the false dark to see what some
overpaid auteur lusts after. We go on because of the
lack of distance applause lends to distance—we clap
not so much to judge as to be that other character,
the one offstage who knows the most—therefore most hurt,
pleased or estranged. Applauding applause. One day a while
before he died, you came over with him. Annie was napping
in her crib and he touched her head and said
sleep well honey. I wanted to cheer him for going on
like that, for blessing my child when he knew he was dying—
and when the raft hit the swells, one after the other;
they held on and prayed and God laughed, God gave them a hand.
That was what God liked most, circling in his capsule,
when they beamed the messages out on the great radio telescopes—
We're here, here's a picture of us third from the sun,
here's D.N.A., a human baby—and a V for peace!
He sent them his holy static, from all the way back
to the Bang, when he first thought of it, the sound of clapping,
on the seventh day, as he sat back, as he rested.

■

At Last

I always fall in love with tired
women. It seems I have the
time. On the blackboard
at the Gay Community
Center it said:
Ladies, we need your
blood. Afterwards
come to the Women's
Coffee House and
have a cup of
coffee. Donation
$1.00. He won't
be complaining
about his big
toe that hurts.
The man who
died last
night. The Death
Squad has taken
him away. I thought
of all the clothes
that guy must've
had. Now no one
can stand to
wear them. I use
Central America
& Southeast
Asia to ease
my mind. Pauline
Kael says that's
squalid. We live

in a culture of
vanishing men.
What is the difference.
Vincent's big joke
is his five-year
membership to
a video club.
They got him on
the phone at the
hospital. He
didn't know
how to say
one year
would probably
do just fine.
It's still hard
to pass up
a bargain. Another
thin man does
a nightclub
act—he does
show tunes
to the horror
of his visiting
friends. He'll
take it on
the road once
he gets better.
At last he knows
what he wants
to do! Jimmy Wayne's
family says Well,
that's what you
get. But I get
something dif-
ferent. What I
do at my desk

is always different
from what I do
on my bed. I was
watching the dif-
ference last
week. This week
I'm different
again. Is it because
of windows that
I think the
day's square
and life is
shaped like
a train. The big
buds outside
my window
make me think
I'm outside
of life because
I can watch
her change
and she can't
see me. You'd
think I'd be
grateful for
my vision. It is
complex. A dance
of images gates
and branches
across buildings
statues windows
firescapes and
creeping cats.
Honey, life
is a blast
and I am
part of it

but you're
separate
from me.
It's how you
want it. The radio
starts up
and I nearly
lose my style.
I opened my heart to
you and now
I feel like
an open wound.
I put my arms
around you
I thought
you felt
great. I called
it heaven
one day

disturbing
once the
train moved

now nothing's
the same.

■

FRANKIE PAINO

For David

On the way to see a friend
who might have died like Keats,
her lungs like his consumed to lace,
I pass them, a nimbus of women
in starched white gowns
surrounding the door to David's room.

Each day they whisper, flip coins,
decide who must bring his dinner in.
They are afraid to breathe his air
and must go home dreading night sweats,
scales registering less of them each day.

Sometimes I see him in the moments
when the door swings open, closed.
He's beautiful, a Caravaggio Cupid,
dark hair, darker eyes, curved
shoulder blades hinting of wings.

Most often he stares out the window
across the valley just beginning to blossom,
as if somewhere in the puzzle
of bare branches lies the reason
why he's left alone, his body collapsing
in on itself like the building he saw
dynamited on Public Square, or the final

moments of a star. In Michigan,
a man driving home sees a dog
cowering at the center of the road,
swerves into the path of a semi.

On the news I see his shattered
windshield. It resembles, in the light
of setting sun, bright pools of blood.

Another world, my friend's room,
heart-shaped balloons tied to her bedrails,
air perfumed with tiger lilies, yellow roses,
baby's-breath. From her fourth-floor window
we watch a helicopter setting down
in a baseball diamond, the only open ground

for miles. It has crossed some distance
we can only imagine, delivers to a waiting ambulance
a chest no larger than a picnic basket,
its sides inscribed with red crosses.

Then, in a flurry of dust and dead leaves
the copter rises, its canary yellow frame
disappearing, she says, like a dream
she can no longer believe in.
At twenty, I saw a boy vanish beneath
the frozen surface of Lake Erie,
his breath suspended in the frigid air.

I remember how the ice zigzagged under me
as I reached out, pulled him towards light,
and my mother's disbelief
when I told her, how pale she was, and angry.

My friend, too, is surprised,
says I'm impulsive, foolish.
She cannot understand, as I believe David does,
how some things are worth risking everything for,
even the love, however brief, of a stranger.

■

MOLLY PEACOCK

Commands of Love

The tragedy of a face in pain
is how little you can do for it
because it is so closed. Having lain

outlined in knives, afraid to move,
it cannot move and therefore cannot love.
This is why we say it is a mask,

for the face is so frozen by hurt and fear
it is unable to ask for help.
You can do nothing but stay near.

This is why we hover over those in pain
doing things unasked for and unwanted,
hoping simply with our bodies to cover pain

as if to protect it. Better to go away.
But by asking for help pain is erased,
for the face opens to say what it has to say

and a beauty of concentration overcomes it.
The pain is saying outwardly what it is.
The help it asks for is what overcomes it.

Help me on with this dress.
Get me a glass of water.
Look, I've made a mess.

Both the face of pain and the face of the one
riveted to it in relief believe there's still
something to get, something to be done.

■

FELICE PICANO

Three Men Speak to Me

i. Tony

That summer we rode giant white Frisbees
over the surf, gliding an eighth of an inch
over sand, seventy-five feet at a slide—
we were like gods of the sea. Shaun moved
to the West Coast for good, while Kelly bought
yards of white muslin to hang in the house.
At night it was lighted like the inside
of a skull. White muslin, white pillows, white
everything! It was the summer of, the
year of, the decade-return of designed
China-white! I wondered what my hair
would look like gone white . . . When it happened
Peter was gone, Vinnie was sick. I only
needed six days—never knew what hit me.

ii. David

They would stand outside the shop on Bleecker
Street and look in at me while I checked
bills of lading. Some waved. Few came in. It
was summer again but my breezy gray
blouson was long-sleeved to cover the spots.
Bad for business: not that I cared. Only
I counted. Every day I would stare into
scores of brass and silver-gilt mirrors
around me for sale, from France, "the real stuff"
George said, and see myself shrink, age by
the hour. Just two years before I'd been a star
in a French porno flick about jaded New

York—the toast of Paree! If you cared to ask
I'd tell you how bitter it tasted. Not
my life, which I loved, not the ups, fists,
dicks that I'd spun on, but this kind of end.
I'd never asked for anything special, had I?
Lived on almost nothing. Never had a lover.
Never made trouble . . . I especially
hated it when my anus began to cave in.
I should have gone to live in France in Sixty-
Eight, like I'd planned to.

iii. Sheldon

Writing a will was the difficult part—
asking next-door neighbors to witness.
The way he pulled back in his doorway, I
could tell he smelled death on my breath.
I'd always minted my mouth, always
ready to kiss my Prince when he arrived.
He never did. I'd worked on my muscles,
dressed well, went to the right discos, bars, clubs,
waiting. Instead I was kidnapped and robbed—
Then *this!* Because I was in medicine
I knew all the signs: no one knew what I had—
the fevers, fatigue, breath like a sewer.
I sat with my lawyer as he handed
'round the will to first her, then him to sign.
They tried to make it light. Sweet of them.
But what did they know . . . What I dread most is
when my relatives from Wyoming go through
my flat. Ask them to be careful. I have
eighteen thousand dollars' worth of rare Ming
ware, collected in decades as I haunted
the aisles at Southeby's, attended every
auction: it was all I ever loved.

■

After the Funerals

After the funerals, the questions arise
vested, rep-tied, quieter than usual, yet
no less intense. Lately, we have become expert
in final symptoms, accomplice-interns of signs.

And all of us have lost—again. Cragged wrecks
or balding sleek, we boys that middle-age chased
in vain, gather in sophisticated chapels
in Miesian aeries high above cities we have planned
and played through and paid for, deciphering

Future suicides or bodies in revolt in the terror
of a glance we once yearned for in fantasy, romance.
Yes, it is clear that males in droves have died before
—died in junglesdemonstrationsflaming planes.
Yes, it is true that, no matter how arch or sissy

The surface, to be a man is to live hot and hard
to slam against concrete edges, to exit in the
strings of a parachute's noose (who knotted?)
and that we, the questioning survivors, are simply,
so far, the elusive fortunate. Or the wily.

Yet . . . after the hospital vigils, the memorials
I sometimes recall August days gilded
like forever when, stepping off the dancefloor
spilling rhythm, even our sweat was silver.

■

Because he'd always considered himself an artist
it wasn't easy to ignore the appearance
of purple spots on his legs. At first he thought
them garish—violets ought not spatter
a perfect tan. Then he became intrigued
with their shapes: broken chains, wadded dollars,
insect stages previously unrecorded.
He had often burned to portray life. Talent
eluded his need. His ambition broke into spite.
As others around him risked—and ascended
he frittered in bathhouses, in coffee shops, jawing.

It was only months later—describing
his Royal, his unasked for, tattoos—grown
now to foliage—that he learned the truth—
how the Dark Angel had heard of his wishes
finally, remembered his name, checked,
and discovered he was scarcely required;
how that Ineffable Aesthete and Joker
had made good for decades of failure,
and let a dank graceless virus develop
artistic to the last, upon
the blank waiting photoplate of his life.

■

STANLEY PLUMLY

Pityriasis Rosea

We say the blood rose, meaning it came to the surface
like a bruise, which comes from outside, blue, in a small violence
a stone, a brush against the table, the punishment of riches;
or meaning the deep object, the blood rose, which is artifice,
since in nature what to look for is color neutral, mallow,
a little pale, like florals years on the canvas, themselves
a kind of nature now with the light and dust in the room's
atmosphere; or meaning the viral air picked out this blood
to rise like the rash after sex, which darkly pollinates
the skin, delicate, in a rush of the blood returning, like
a weight of ash, to the heart, except that here it comes
in petal-, sepal-sized extrusions, but softer, like embarrassment,
the flaw a fire-leak in the blood, hectic, risen, flush
on the upper body with passion, intermission, mouth of the kiss.

The sickle, the scythe in the blood, which means to sweep
the tide of its impurities, like a sword in the wave, cuts, fails,
rises like a thorn—we say this too is the blood burning clean.
But only the wren flower, yarrow, or the nettle will heal the old
wound or the dry bleeding, which made the flesh blush even to itself
and the boy on the hillside, working in a fever of the summer
against the wire of undergrowth, walks away, because his hands
wouldn't close. The raw rose on the back of my hand is a sign
of the season, something in the air, like pollen and the garden
phlox we let grow wild, sick purple, pink, what a child or a man
might worry meant corruption of the purest part, the blood,
which is immortal and fire on the river running backwards, forwards
in a wind, dangerous, anonymous as any other part of ourselves
passed on, scattered, or poured back into the earth.

■

JAMES PURDY

I Have Told You Your
Hands Are Salt

I have seen your hands asleep
the veins are talking to me as you lie
your hands are white as salt
they invite the lips and even the teeth
the salt-white hands that lie on the quilt
command a terrible kiss.

■

J. M. REGAN

This Morning's Lecture
Is of Ionized

This morning's lecture is of ionized
stem cells and the immuno-compromised.
Two fragile biologies, we lunch near
Dumbarton, make unsafe love on a shore
of the Potomac where the fish kills wash
up daily and the kissing bugs flourish.
Your eyes keep the regulation black-out;
I look forward to the final fall-out.

So does the sea, also free of worry,
let the moon unloose, over and over
from its cave of knives, the ruthless ova.
They bloom as red as algae in July;
they are the megadead—oh dysthymic!
oh vector! this noble epidemic!

■

Adrienne Rich

In Memoriam

A man walking on the street
feels unwell   has felt unwell
all week, a little   Yet the flowers crammed
in pots on the corner: furled anemones:
he knows they open
burgundy, violet, pink, amarillo
all the way to their velvet cores
The flowers hanging over the wall: fuchsias:
each tongues, staring   all of a fire:
the flowers   He who has
been happy oftener than sad
carelessly happy, well   oftener than sick
one of the lucky   is thinking about death
and its music   about poetry
its translations of his life

And what good will it do you
to go home and put on the Mozart Requiem?
Read Keats?   How will culture cure you?

Poor, unhappy

unwell culture   what can it sing or say
six weeks from now, to you?

Give me your living hand   If I could take the hour
death moved into you   undeclared, unnamed
—even if sweet, if I could take that hour
between my forceps   tear at it like a monster
wrench it out of your flesh   dissolve its shape in quicklime
and make you well again

no, not again

but still . . .

■

MARK RUDMAN

Nerves

I'm not really nervous since John warned me about Toxic Shock
    Syndrome,
I'm content with the odds against it.

The jell in these super absorbent diapers is what brings it on,
he says, and, as is well known, Tampons—

I just read the warning again on the box.
If the child saturates this splendidly bulkless diaper in the night

he can loose the jell, which, if it soaks
into his skin, can kill him.

How much are we willing to pay for convenience?
I'm not nervous about catching AIDS from my infected friends,

a simple hug can't bring it on and my friends
are fastidious and considerate.

I've known people who were so afraid of germs
they brought their own boiled forks and knives

when they came to dinner—whose first words
on entering the door were always—"don't kiss me!"

And as to the spread of Lyme Disease, we've been instructed
to walk with pant cuffs tucked into shoes;

who would bother, really, when so few cases
have been reported in this state—

but when my son smashes the wiffle ball deep
into the tall wet grass around the house

I hesitate—before letting go and plunging in after it. . . .
When I drive his babysitter home this dark summer noon

she tells of how she likes the cold, hates the heat,
the insects and scorpions it breeds,

(I've never seen one this far north),
says if hell is always hot then maybe cold is—heaven . . .

I'm not nervous, merely apprehensive.
It's a kind of voodoo, a way

of controlling fate by inviting the worst
to happen in the form of made-up fears.

My son will still put anything into his mouth,
a fly swatter for instance,

and I play on his fear of bugs to get him to wash his hands
after he uses a public toilet

by saying the germs are like invisible bugs,
nervous that I might stir up phobias.

I'm vigilant where preservatives are concerned,
but lose the battle of Nutrasweet by drinking Diet Coke in his
        presence—

thanks to Alice Miller I can't deny him several swigs—
and I forcibly repress my fears that it does cause cancer
        in humans.

Then a friend offers that she nearly died last night
from a high fever and she thinks now maybe Nutrasweet
        brought it on

because she never drinks diet soda.
My father drank at least a gallon of diet soda a day

and he didn't die of cancer: He merely lost his mind.
He feared that nothing natural could kill him.

Now that I think of it, the people I mentioned
each turned their cheeks so far to the side I thought

they would come off their necks—
the same way my father, in his madness toward the end,

turned his cheek away from my lips
when I went to kiss him.

■

The Second Law

Beside the bed I watch
      His hindered face
The dented cheeks lifting
      And falling,
Scarcely perceived, with the stoking,
      The curbed

Breathing. I hold a mug of black
      Coffee fresh
From the nurse's station, heat
      Is working its
Arduous way through the glazed
      China wall

To my cold hand. Soon
      It is too hot
To hold; I put it down
      And I take
The colder hand in mine.
      And I wonder

If it is taking any warmth
      From mine
Or if his chill alone
      Is oozing
Through the wall of our grip, our
      Holding on. I

Stand outside the bars through which
      The gaze clings;
And the stubble crowning the sheet;
      And the jailed
Knowing, letting him, letting him
      Go.

■

RON SCHREIBER

recovery

your arms & legs are shrunken
mush, the muscles gone—but

already—as you begin to eat—
the arms start to come back.

you have a walker for your legs
& you walk to the toilet

across your room. except for
the weekend (which is now) you

have help: a woman from PT.
now the floor is badly under-

staffed. you're on your own
—with visits from your parents,

Nancy, Suzanne. I come twice
a day, my routine pegged to your

"recovery." at home I'm getting
prepared: yesterday I cleaned

the guest room, where you'll
stay; this morning I've raised

the storms & put the screens in.
the cats huddle at the windows &

listen to birds they haven't
heard all winter. the Easter

cactus blooms in your new room
if you do indeed "recover" this week:

bright, gaudy red flower, full
in the sun, as wide as an arm.

■

the   hardest

that's what I've been saying
for three weeks; but this

(so far) is it: watching John
start to die, his face not so

much in pain as frowning, not
wanting to let go, his body

frail beyond simple weakness,
his spirit not yet broken,

his eyes puzzled. (:   why John?
why me?—questions we've never asked.)

it's like a glacier accelerating,
the town, the whole economy,

the "lifestyle" (as we've been
trivialized) about to be

engulfed in cold.

■

have almost all migrated
now, the Canada geese a

roar of noise, the hawks stopping
over the Cape. all gone

South like the satyrs,
their yellow & black wings

a whoosh of noise. *we*
cannot prevent, the Chinese

sage says (in the passage
my mother sent me from Florida)

the birds of sorrow from
flying over our heads.

I put on my winter clothing
—T-shirt, flannel shirt—

as the weather changes.
but we can refuse (against

the cold comes suddenly into
my body now John is gone)

to let them build nests
(my carts protect me; eyeing

the birds; salivating)
in our hair.

■

John didn't die. he hasn't
died yet. but he's only

rarely coherent, we're
thankful for a smile, a

shard of conversation.
when he screams "no no noo

no no" "go home," we are
glad that he has his voice

back & says actual words
rather than moans. when

he claws at his chest, we
say, "he's trying to use

his hands." today he
may be better, longer

moments of attempted speech.
today he may not

be better. we don't know:
day to day, hour to hour.

it will be short or longer.
his brain will work

or it won't.

■

your life

right now it's all I care about
& you're going to lose it

(wrong head, I know, but it's
late & I'm scared & tired).

first there's your health: I
want you to have it, you were

exhausted & sun-dazed when I
brought you back from the hospital

—after stopping to get your drugs—
& you were sleeping when I called

downstairs just now. I am tired
beyond anything my body tells me

is fatigue. & when you're sick,

when I look into your tired, lovely
eyes, I want you well. right now

I'm trying to find the railroad cap
I lost on the long flight wait

in Florida last winter, when I was
there & you were home & healthy,

& put it on my head firm & screw it
on. I want you to get back your

health or at least its shimmering
surface. right now.

■

he slept through the night:
four to eight—no pain

when he sleeps. I slept:
eight to eleven; eleven

to three; three to four;
up at six. worked.

typed two documents,
played solitaire. mailed

letter at the corner
store, where I got cig-

arettes but no paper
(they didn't have one).

came back. played soli-
taire. till John screamed

just now, & I gave him
a morphine capsule.

he's on his stomach.
wet? I don't know; I

didn't turn him over.
I love you, he said.

I'd said that to him
first, and—let it go now;

I'm all right. I *am*
all right, whatever

that means, it means
ready. & I told him so

& he understands me. it's
time for the others to

tell him too.

■

MAUREEN SEATON

White Balloon

To love something you know will die is holy.
Kaddish, AIDS Memorial,
New York, 1987

The air is gravid with life,
the cloudless sky swells
with souls, ascending.

I'm in charge of one young soul
tied to my wrist
with a string that won't break.

St. Veronica's, the end of June:
You weep beside me, hold
a candle steadily near the flame.

Earlier we were two ladies
shopping on Broadway. I recall
your wire of a body,

the delicate arc of ribs
and small breast above—this
as you quick-changed

in search of something radical,
feminine. Your terror of pink
amused me. You said:

Don't tell anyone
of this sudden reversal. I said:
I will, but I'll change your name.

Linda, it's the letting go
that terrifies: the night air
alive with rising ghosts,

the cries of strong men
grieving in each other's arms,
the ease with which we love.

■

CHARLIE SMITH

Beauty Kills

In Virginia
I stalled a while watching a bay horse
crop grass in a small lot
near the highway. Blue spidergrass
and bitterweed flourished among piles
of rusted implements, among a hay rake with tines
like the delicate rib bones of an ancient fish and old lumber.
I thought, the way one can, that the new loss
of your love
might become a permanent sadness,
and I was sad
because I knew it wouldn't. We had not lingered
one evening in Virginia
to watch a bay mare, her coat roughed
already for winter, crop the sparse bahaia grass
in a cluttered lot—so it wasn't memory
that touched my sadness, though
what amplified the loss
was ample enough. And it wasn't
what might have been,
because I couldn't picture you
in that place, where a sly breeze
pretended to steal the smallest leaves, and the horse,
I saw, was old, and lame. We imagined children
and hard work, waking by the lake
in Michigan, but we got
to none of these. I read a passage once
about a form of chastity
that acknowledged,
but abstained from pursuing,
the beauty of the world, and I thought of the afternoon

I turned to you on the beach at Pamet Roads
and saw your face for an instant
shining like all I would ever love
or had ever loved, and though the moment passed
like one of the thin green waves
skittering in, I knew I would give myself away, I knew
I had already given myself away
to what I saw shining in you, that I would make the mistake
I had made before,
and would probably make again, of believing
your face, your voice, your
history, was the thing
itself,
and so wind up lost. They say it isn't the squalor
that kills, it's the beauty. It's what—and all—
on a bright day
when as we watch the light tremble in sheets
on the pond, we surrender to,
and so go dumbly down,
and are ruined,
and return from dazed and chastened,
as a callow boy caught thieving in an orchard
will glance at the bootless blue sky,
at the treasure of ripe fruit
filling his shirt, and descend
into the irate farmer's world,
unable to explain anything—
not his theft, or himself,
or what makes him what he is.

■

WILLIAM JAY SMITH

Journey to the Interior

He has gone into the forest,
to the wooded mind in wrath;
he will follow out the nettles
and the bindweed path.

He is torn by tangled roots,
he is trapped by mildewed air;
he will feed on alder shoots
and on fungi. In despair

he will pursue each dry creek-bed,
each hot white gully's rough raw stone
till heaven opens overhead
a vast jawbone

and trees around grow toothpick-thin
and a deepening dustcloud swirls about
and every road leads on within
and none leads out.

■

LAUREL SPEER

Mama Rosanna's Last Bead-Clack

I'm sitting on my couch saying my rosary. I haven't
been inside a Catholic church in 14 years, but this
is something I learned early and give up never.
It's my ritual when I wake up choking. I drink hot tea;
I don't take in food; I listen; I say my decades;
I pray; I look at TV. My color isn't good; I'm losing
weight; my lungs fill up. I'm old; I'm used up;
I haven't lived a good life. I don't go out;
I don't wash. I've seen pictures on TV and know now
I'm one of them. I'm afraid. People will come
to my house and burn my bedding. Lamb of God, kill me.

■

ELIZABETH SULLAM

To Joseph

Latex drips over New York skyscrapers,
over the wind-creped surface of the Hudson;
cathedral bells are fastened, the portals
                                    purple-draped.

Night begs for clemency against the talons
of the perennial Sphinx, I for your undimming
aesthetic eyes, Antinous smile, resurrection
of your soul and flesh. Once you spoke
of another kind of love. Woman and old friend
I understood your choice, and our friendship flourished.

My hands cup your moon-diaphanous smile
while acanthus leaves whisper "mystery, mystery,"
innocent like a child's game a cruel nurse
suddenly interrupts, placid like the renaissance dream
lived among ruined columns and roaming cats.

Your gentle smile that startled Hadrian's eyes
and the Roman stones is nobody's but the dark
fields of asphodels. On Banchi Vecchi Street,
where alone and lonely, Hadrian weeps; on Villa
Giulia's grounds; on courts restored by your unfailing
classic hand, the sky releases a rain of old coins.

■

DAVID TRINIDAD

Driving Back from New Haven

Tim looks at his watch, reaches into his
pocket, takes out a small plastic container
and swallows an AZT pill with a sip of Sprite.
"Poison," he mutters under his breath. I
glance over at him. We haven't talked about
his health the entire trip. "How does it
make you feel?" I ask. "Like I want to live
until they discover a cure," he snaps. We
travel in silence for a while. I stare out
the window at all the green trees on the
Merritt Parkway. Then he says: "I resent
it. I resent that we were not raised with
an acceptance of death. And here it is,
all around us. And I fucking resent it.
I resent that we do not know how to die."

■

X

I have decorated this banner to honor my brother.
Our parents did not want his name used publicly.

From an unnamed child's banner
in the AIDS Memorial Quilt

The earthblue eye of the boatpond smiled at the sky.
I remember looking at you, X, this way,
taking in your color, your light, and I miss you
so. I know,
you are you, and real, standing there in the doorway,
whether dead or whether living, real. —Then Y
said, "Who will remember me three years after I die?
What is there for my eye
to read then?"
The lamb should not have given
his wool.
He was so small. At the end, X, you were so small.
Playing with a stone
on your bedspread at the edge of the ocean.

■

W i l l i ,   H o m e

In memory

Last night, just before sleep, this: a bright
daffodil
lying in bed, with the sheet pulled up to its chin.
Willi, did I ever know you? The shine
in the lamplight!   of your intelligent glasses,
round and humorous.
Did I ever know myself? When I
start bullshitting I see your eyebrows fly . . . This book
is dedicated to Willi,
whom I do not know,

whom I know. The words in my head
this morning
(these words came from an angel):
"It's too late to say goodbye.
And there are never enough goodbyes."
I know: the daffodil
is me. Brave. Willi's an iris. Brave.
Brave. Tall. Home. Deep. Blue.

■

Light
old leaf spine
fish spine bone
green under-the-
ocean light

Big gold fish my
new little father
only a boy
breathing on the window
COME ON OUT,

My eggful of eggs
floating opening
up in your cream, up in
your blood.
Are you sick? Are you well?

*A blood sample will be taken from your
arm with a needle and analyzed in a
laboratory using a test called ELISA
(enzyme-linked immunosorbent assay).
If the ELISA test is positive, a
second test, called Western Blot, will
be run on the same blood sample to
confirm the result.*

The palm of your glove is
powder on my mouth, powder in my fear,
your rough tongue your talk is
warm on the cool hospital-issue
black silk blindfold crackhouse blindfold

you green in the dark tying a rubber
strap around my arm playing the radio
your heavy head, green in the dark,
Are you still in the room?
Are you still in the house?

Then you, Doctor, American doctor
in my dream, you say sincerely,
"You can always go on suicide neutral,
then everyone, from both sides, from his side and her side,
will leave you alone." And

Mother State, you say, "You are not enough.
I am. Eat me, &
I will raise you up. On TV, eat me.
Chew me, gingerly, like chewing ice,
eat me. My America. Eat me."

■

AIDS-Related Complex

I have an earache;
well, not exactly an earache,
but when I pull on it, there
is hurt more than I remember
there having been a few years back.
Aches appear as regular forecasts.

I need the dogs to hide inside
their love on a Tuesday night,
weary from being helplessly small.
They are unaware of change, only
how the bags of food arrived
as that evening falls on us
together, with their bodies, one head
on each of my arms, healed beside me.
I don't have to tell them I may
be too decayed for closeness.

True, yes, I have had excesses
though not the excess of many others:
there are always others worse.
But I never was that bad,
so why do I finger my glands
every morning instead of sunlight?

I note they seem like swollen rocks
rearranged by the earth finding new starts,
or the weather's change, or something.
Listen, I'm too good for this image,
an unlikely candidate for everything
that is allowed to happen around me,

especially strangers making the most
of the dark and smokey air. Desperate
to talk about it, we can't. We have
seen Par-ee, and the farm just about
sucks the teats of rotting cattle.
It's too tragic to fear a kiss—
oh the tongues I receded simpering
to the end of my throat in love
with escapes from routine smooches.
Now I can't, so every weakening
is followed by *angst* that last
night's tryst carried death's
seminal saliva we were right to fear.

We suspected all along. The ticks
in our minds toll that it can't
so it could; and if it did
(we remember running past nights
for some burning, communicable
dark mare sweating to our fires)
we'd have had taken from us all
our merits from hard tests of survival.
We embrace anyhow, but shouldn't we
be able to counsel out the romantic
who revels inside these foolish hearts?
We can't have it any other way:
enraptured by the rhapsodies, we are
twisted by a distorted treble
that dominates our unwanted dawns.
The beast can't be killed for some
time, only outlasted like a memory.

My constant cold: a certain part of it.
Half the population has been exposed; then
how much longer might it take for us
to meet the other suffering half, all
turned into lepers dying with a secret

the times don't allow us to mention.
The best of us may be going, timidly,
like yesterday's Jews falling silent
on brothers who, turned away while again
praying to be saved on these shores, weren't.
It's always the choice of lords with power.
Despised in their lies, we can't risk a loud
scream for our very lives at stake, replete
with all the iconoclasm we'd composed ourselves,
revealed here in the less than unapologetic air.
We batten down double-edged shadows from which
we perceive that we're safe in a crowd
to dance to our own goings under.
There, there
we may rockabye through, possible survivors,
recalling it wasn't as bad as it is.

■

MILLER WILLIAMS

Thinking About Bill,
Dead of AIDS

We did not know the first thing about
how blood surrenders to even the smallest threat
when old allergies turn inside out,

the body rescinding all its normal orders
to all defenders of flesh, betraying the head,
pulling its guards back from all its borders.

Thinking of friends afraid to shake your hand,
we think of your hand shaking, your mouth set,
your eyes drained of any reprimand.

Loving, we kissed you, partly to persuade
both you and us, seeing what eyes had said,
that we were loving and were not afraid.

If we had had more, we would have given more.
As it was we stood next to your bed,
stopping, though, to set our smiles at the door.

Not because we were less sure at the last.
Only because, not knowing anything yet,
we didn't know what look would hurt you least.

■

Acknowledgments

There are so many men and women to thank for helping with the delivery of this book—beginning, of course, with all the poets who believed it would happen, and in particular: David Craig Austin, Henri Cole, and the Academy of American Poets for their unending support; J. D. McClatchy for his recommendations; Edward Field and Tom Sleigh for carrying the message to those who didn't know; Phillis Levin for early and sustained wishing; Marilyn Hacker for turning me on to Olga Broumas; Olga Broumas for turning me on to how a line goes supple; Felice Picano for staying so long on the phone and reminding me that laughing is part of it; Mark Doty for his wonderful criticism and company during July in Little Compton; Paul Monette for being compassionately and importantly on the front line and for his valuable suggestions; Adrienne Rich for reentering my life in a way that makes perfect sense; and Jean Valentine, who kept giving me another reason when I would run out of them.

Also special thanks and love to Joseph Danisi, Jeff Jelly, Kate Colleran, Kirk Kerber, Christopher Eldredge, Kevin Farrell, Brian Boyle, Tom Bywaters, Anita Wagenvoord, Michael Schwartz, John Wetter, Carl Morse, Joan Larkin, Maggie Valentine, Judith Baumel and the Poetry Society of America; Now and Then Productions; Gregory Kolovakis and the PEN Emergency Fund for Writers and Editors With AIDS; the word-processing staff at Fulbright Jaworski & Reavis McGrath; Alfred A. Knopf, W. W. Norton, Random House, Viking Press, the Pittsburgh University Press, David R. Godine, Inc., Alice James Books, The University of Georgia Press, and St. Martin's Press for waiving all permissions fees; Mark

McCauslin, Crown's wise production editor; Linda Kocur, book designer; Bob Collett and Joan Denman, production supervisors; friends of Bill W. and in particular Xena, for telling me the truth, and Peter, for putting it simply; Richard, for teaching me the difference between loneliness and solitude and, finally, thanks to Linsey Abrams for help with the introduction, Mary Jane Sullivan for a meticulous job proofreading the manuscript, my agent, Stephanie Laidman, who never lost hope—and to my editor, David Groff, who kept renewing mine.

Contributors' Notes

David Craig Austin was executive secretary and editor of *Poetry Pilot* at the Academy of American Poets and now works at Gay Men's Health Crisis. His poems have appeared in *Black Warrior Review, Poetry East,* and *The Yale Review.* Mr. Austin lives in New York City, where he also reviews for *The New York Native.*

Wendy Barker was awarded an N.E.A. Fellowship in poetry in 1986. She has contracted with Indiana University Press to write a book with the working title *Death Blows, Life Blows: Women of Letters in Nineteenth-Century America.*

Robin Behn's first book of poems, *Paper Bird,* won the Associated Writing Programs Award Series of Poetry and was published by Texas Tech University Press. Her poems have appeared in such journals as *The American Poetry Review, Poetry, The Georgia Review,* and *Field.* She teaches in the M.F.A. Program at the University of Alabama.

Marvin Bell lives in Iowa City, Iowa, and Port Townsend, Washington. His many books include seven collections of poetry from Atheneum, which published his *New and Selected Poems* in 1987.

David Bergman lives in Baltimore, Maryland, where he teaches at Towson State University. He is the recipient of the 1985 George Elliston Poetry Prize for his book *Cracking the Code* (Ohio State University Press, 1985) and has just completed editing *Reported Sightings: John Ashbery's Art Chronicles 1957–1987* (Knopf, 1988).

Michael Blumenthal is a professor of English and American Literature at Harvard University. He is the author of the poetry collections *Days We Would Rather Know* and *Against Romance,* both from Viking.

Philip Booth's *Relations: Selected Poems, 1950–1985* was published by Viking Penguin in 1988.

Walta Borawski is the author of *Sexually Dangerous Poet* (Good Gay Poets, 1984) and lives in Cambridge, Massachusetts.

Olga Broumas's first book, *Beginning With O,* was selected by Stanley Kunitz for the Yale Younger Poets Award in 1977. Her latest book of poems is *The Little Mariner* from Copper Canyon Press. A recipient of Guggenheim and N.E.A. fellowships, she resides in Provincetown, Massachusetts.

Michael Burkard's books of poetry include *Fictions From the Self* (W. W. Norton, 1988), *The Fires They Kept* (Metro Book Co., 1986), and *Ruby for Grief* (University of Pittsburgh, 1981). He is married to the painter Mary Alice Johnston and is currently a publicist for the Rome Art and Community Center.

Michael Cadnum's sixth collection of poetry, *By Evening,* won the 1989 Owl Creek Book Award. His work has been included in many anthologies, and among numerous awards he holds a fellowship from the National Endowment for the Arts.

Kevin Jeffery Clarke attended Goddard College in Vermont and City College in New York. His poems have appeared in *Antaeus, The Hudson Review,* and *The Paris Review,* as well as Dennis Cooper's anthology *Coming Attractions.* He works as a copywriter with Taylor & Francis in New York and is at work on his first book of poems.

Henri Cole has served as director of the Academy of American Poets and is the author of *The Marble Queen* (Atheneum). His poems have appeared in *Antaeus, The Nation,* and *Poetry.* He lives in New York City.

Robert Cording teaches English at Holy Cross College in Worcester, Massachusetts. His first book, *Life-List,* won the Ohio University Press Award, and his poems have appeared in *The New Yorker, American Scholar,* and many other journals.

Alfred Corn's new book of poems is *The West Door,* and he has previously published four books of poetry, all from Viking Press. He has received a National Endowment of the Arts award, the George Dillion and Blumenthal prizes from *Poetry* magazine, and a Fulbright. He lives in New York City.

Robert Creeley is best known as a poet but has also published a wide range of prose. Recent books include *Collected Poems, 1945–1975, Collected Prose,* and *Memory Gardens.* He was editor of *The Black Mountain Review.* Mr. Creeley's poem "Plague" was written expressly for this book.

William Dickey has published ten books of poetry, most recently *Brief Lives* (Heyeck Press, 1985) and *The King of the Golden River* (Pterodactyl Press, 1986); the latter book won the San Francisco Bay Area Book Reviewers' poetry award for 1986.

Deborah Digges's second book of poems, *Late in the Millennium,* and a book of non-fiction, *Fugitive Spring,* are due out from Knopf in late 1989. Her first book, *Vesper Sparrows* (Atheneum), won the Delmore Schwartz Memorial Poetry Prize from N.Y.U. Her poems have appeared in *Antaeus, The New Yorker,* and other magazines.

Melvin Dixon is the author of *Change of Territory* (Callaloo Poetry Series, University Press of Virginia, 1983). His most recent fiction appears in *Men on Men 2: An Anthology of Gay Fiction,* edited by George Stambolian (New American Library, 1988). The recipient of fellowships in creative writing from the National Endowment of the Arts (1984) and the New York Foundation for the Arts (1988), he currently lives in Manhattan.

Tim Dlugos's poems have been published in four collections, most recently *Entre Nous,* and in *The Paris Review, Bomb,* and many other literary journals. He is a board member of The Poetry Project at St. Mark's Church-in-the-Bowery, and a contributing editor of *Christopher Street* magazine. He currently is pursuing graduate studies at Yale Divinity School.

Mark Doty teaches in the M.F.A. Program at Vermont College. His book of poetry, *Turtle, Swan,* was published in 1987 by David Godine, and the title poem won a Pushcart Prize that same year and brought a N.E.A. Fellowship. His new book is called *Bethlehem in Broad Daylight.* He lives in Montpelier, Vermont.

Carol Ebbecke was born in 1963 in Minneapolis. She received her B.F.A. from Bowling Green State University, and is presently completing her M.A. in Creative Writing at Syracuse University, where she edits the graduate literary magazine and writes freelance.

Eve Ensler is a widely published poet and editor of *Central Park* magazine. She just finished an adaptation of her play, *The Depot,* for a film to be directed by Joanne Woodward and starring Shirley Knight. She is a founding member of CANDU, a grass-roots peace group in the Chelsea section of Manhattan, where she lives. Ms. Ensler's poem "To Richard" was written for this book.

Edward Field has won the Lamont Award, the Shelley Memorial Award, and the Rome Prize of the American Academy and Institute of Arts and Letters. The documentary film *To Be Alive,* for which he wrote the narration, won an Academy Award. His latest book is

New and Selected Poems (Sheep Meadow Press). Mr. Field lives in New York City.

Gary Fincke is Writing Program Director at Susquehanna University. His third collection of poetry, *The Days of Uncertain Health,* is just out from Lynx House Press. His poems have appeared in *Poetry Northwest, The Georgia Review, Poetry,* and *Prairie Schooner.* His new book, *Handing the Self Back,* will be published by Green Tower Press in early 1990.

Allen Ginsberg's most recent works include *Collected Poems 1947– 1980, White Shroud,* and *Annotated Notes to "Howl."* He is currently Distinguished Professor of English at Brooklyn College and spends each summer and spring teaching at the Naropa Institute in Boulder, Colorado.

Brad Gooch is the author of a book of poems, *The Daily News* (Z Press); a collection of short stories, *Jailbait* (Seahorse Press); and a novel, *Scary Kisses* (Putnam). He is presently at work on a biography of Frank O'Hara, which Knopf will publish.

David Groff is an editor at Crown Publishers, where he worked with Michael Klein on *Poets for Life: 76 Poets Respond to AIDS.* His poems have appeared in *Poetry, The American Poetry Review, The Georgia Review,* and *The Mississippi Review,* his short stories in *Christopher Street* and *Men on Men 2,* and his articles in *7 Days.*

Thom Gunn was born in 1929 in England and raised there too. He came to the U.S. in 1954, which was the year his first book of poems, *Fighting Terms,* was published. His most recent work is *The Passages of Joy,* published by Farrar Straus & Giroux in 1982. Mr. Gunn lives in San Francisco.

Marilyn Hacker's books include *Love, Death, and the Changing of the Seasons* (Arbor House, 1986) and *Assumptions* (Knopf, 1985). Her *Presentation Piece* (Viking, 1975) won the National Book Award. From 1982 to 1986, Ms. Hacker served as editor of the feminist literary review *13th Moon.*

Rachel Hadas, a Guggenheim Fellow in Poetry, 1988–89, teaches English at Rutgers University. She is the author of three books of poems, most recently *A Son From Sleep* (Wesleyan University Press). Her fourth collection, *Pass It On,* will be published by Princeton University Press in Spring 1989.

Joseph Hansen is the author of *Backtrack, Bradstetter and Others,* and *Steps Going Down,* all mysteries. His most recent novel, *Early Graves,* deals specifically with AIDS. "Red Suspenders, Boxes of Cigars" was written especially for this book. Mr. Hansen lives in Los Angeles.

Richard Harteis's latest collection of poetry is *Internal Geography* (Carnegie-Mellon University Press). His newest book is *Training,* a prose account of the New York City Marathon. For the last seventeen years he has been close associate and friend to the poet William Meredith.

Christopher Hewitt has an M.F.A. in Poetry from the University of Iowa and teaches English at Fordham University and John Jay College in Manhattan. His translations of the Romanian poet Nina Cassian have appeared in *The New Yorker,* and his chapbook of poems, *The Infinite Et Cetera,* was published in 1981 by Green River Press.

Daryl Hine has published eight books of poetry, all from Atheneum. From 1968 to 1977 he served as editor of *Poetry* magazine. He lives in Evanston, Illinois.

Edward Hirsch has published three books of poems: *For the Sleepwalkers* (1981), *Wild Gratitude* (1986), and *The Night Parade* (1989), all from Knopf. He teaches at the University of Houston.

Walter Holland graduated from Bard College and earned his M.S. from Columbia University. His poetry has been published in *The George Mason Review* and *Christopher Street.*

Lynda Hull was born in Newark, New Jersey, and has traveled widely. Her first collection of poetry, *Ghost Money,* won the Juniper Prize in 1986 from the University of Massachusetts Press. Her poems have appeared in *The New Yorker, Poetry, The Missouri Review, Antioch Review,* and other journals. She teaches in the M.F.A. Writing Program of Vermont College.

Greg Johnson is an assistant professor of English at the University of Mississippi and the author of *Understanding Joyce Carol Oates* (University of South Carolina Press, 1987) and *Emily Dickinson: Perception and the Poet's Quest* (University of Alabama Press, 1985). His poems have appeared in *The Virginia Quarterly Review, The Georgia Review, Prairie Schooner,* and other literary periodicals.

June Jordan is the author of sixteen books, novels, and collections of poetry. Her novel *His Own Where* was a finalist for the National Book Award in 1972. Her poems, articles, essays, and reviews have appeared in *Ms., The New York Times, The Nation, Essence,* and *Partisan Review.* She is currently a professor of English at SUNY at Stony Brook, where she also serves as Director of The Poetry Center and The Creative Writing Program.

Arnie Kantrowitz is the author of *Under the Rainbow: Growing Up Gay,* an autobiography, and has recently completed a novel, *The Poet of the Body.* He is an associate professor of English at The College of Staten Island, City University of New York.

X. J. Kennedy writes college textbooks for a living, in Bedford, Massachusetts. His first book of verse, *Nude Descending a Staircase* (Doubleday, 1961), received a Lamont Award, and his most recent, *Cross Ties: Selected Poems* (The University of Georgia Press, 1985), a Los Angeles Times Book Award.

Michael Klein is the editor of *Poets for Life: 76 Poets Respond to AIDS*. He attended Bennington College and his poems have appeared in *Black Warrior Review, Boulevard,* and *Pequod.* From 1979 to 1984 he worked as a groom at Belmont Park, where he cared for 1984 Kentucky Derby winner Swale. In 1988 he won the Open Voice Award for Poetry from the Writer's Voice in New York City and is presently enrolled in the M.F.A. Program in Writing at Vermont College. He lives in Brooklyn, New York.

Wayne Koestenbaum is an assistant professor of English at Yale University. His poems have appeared in *The Yale Review, Boulevard,* and other journals. Mr. Koestenbaum also reviews poetry for the *Village Voice, Commonweal,* and *The New York Native.*

Steve Kowit is an animal rights activist and lives and teaches in San Diego. He has translated the political poetry of Pablo Neruda and Ernesto Cardenal. He edited *The Maverick Poets: An Anthology* for Gorilla Press and is the author of a book of poems, *Lurid Confessions* (Carpenter Press).

Michael Lassell is the current managing editor of *L.A. Style* magazine and has worked as a critic and art teacher/writer for the *Times Herald Examiner* and for *LA Weekly.* His poems have appeared in *Poetry LA, The Literary Review, James White Review,* and *Hanging Loose.* His book, *Poems for Lost and Un-Lost Boys* won the Amelia Chapbook Award in 1986, and he has poems in Carl Morse and Joan Larkin's anthology *Gay and Lesbian Poetry in our Time.*

Phillis Levin graduated from Sarah Lawrence College and just published her first book, *Temples, Fields,* which Bin Ramke chose for the University of Georgia Press. She is an associate editor at *Boulevard* magazine and lives in New York City.

Robert Louthan's second book of poetry is *Living in Code* (University of Pittsburgh Press, 1983). He is currently a law student. His poem "Syndrome" was written especially for this book.

Paul Mariah edits and publishes ManRoot Books. He lives in the valley of the moon with fifteen fruit trees in his yard. He is presently reordering and reorganizing his life after losing his lover of fifteen years to AIDS.

Richard McCann's fiction and poetry have appeared in *The Atlantic, Esquire,* and *The Virginia Quarterly Review,* as well as in George Stambolian's *Men on Men 2.* He is currently at work on a novel to be published by Viking/Penguin and has received fellowships from the MacDowell Colony and Yaddo. He co-directs the M.F.A. Program in Creative Writing at The American University.

J. D. McClatchy is the author of two books of poems, *Scenes From Another Life* (1981) and *Stars Principal* (1986), and a collection of essays, *White Paper* (1969). He has taught at Yale and Princeton, and lives in New York City.

Heather McHugh lives in Maine summers and falls, teaches in Seattle winters and springs. The poems here are from the collection *Shades* just published—like its companion volume *To the Quick*—by Wesleyan University Press.

James Merrill is the author of nine books of poems, which have won him two National Book Awards (for *Nights and Days* and *Mirabell*), the Bollingen Prize in Poetry (for *Braving the Elements*), and the Pulitzer Prize in 1977 (for *Divine Comedies*). His new volume, *The Inner Room,* was published by Knopf. A book of prose, *Recititive,* edited by J. D. McClatchy, was published by North Point Press. Mr. Merrill is a member of the American Institute of Arts and Letters.

Paul Monette is the author of four novels, including *Taking Care of Mrs. Carroll* and *The Gold Diggers.* He has also published three books of poems, the most recent being *Love Alone: 18 Elegies for Rog* (1988). His AIDS memoir, *Borrowed Time,* chronicles the life and meaningless death of his beloved friend, Roger Horwitz.

Honor Moore lives in Kent, Connecticut, and has just published *Memoir,* a book of poems (Chicory Blue Press). She is presently working on a biography of her grandmother, the artist Margaret Sargent, which will be published by Viking Penguin this year.

Carol Muske teaches at U.S.C. and has a fourth book of poems, *Applause,* and a novel, *Dear Digby,* published in April 1989.

Eileen Myles served as Artistic Director at St. Marks Poetry Project from 1984 to 1986. Her books include *The Irony of the Leash, A Fresh Young Voice From the Plains, Sappho's Boat,* and *The Real Drive.*

Frankie Paino is currently working toward her M.F.A. at Vermont College. Her work has appeared in *Poetry Miscellany, Whiskey Island,* and *Oxford* magazine.

Molly Peacock's third collection of poetry, *Take Heart,* was published in spring 1989 by Random House, which also published her *Raw*

Heaven (1984). She has received awards from, among other organizations, The Ingram Merrill Foundation (1981 and 1986) and The New York Foundation for the Arts (1985).

Felice Picano is the author of six novels, a collection of short stories, and a collection of poetry. *Ambidextrous,* a first volume of memoirs, is forthcoming, as is a novel, *To the Seventh Power,* which William Morrow will publish.

Stanley Plumly's most recent book was *Summer Celestial,* a collection of poems published by Ecco. "Pityriasis Rosea" will be appearing in a new collection to be published in late 1989. Mr. Plumly teaches at the University of Maryland.

James Purdy's novels include *Malcolm, The Nephew,* and *Eustace Chisholm and the Works.* His most recent novel is *In the Hollow of His Hand. Garments the Living Wear* will be published in 1989.

J. M. Regan was educated at Georgetown and CUNY. A former writing instructor at CUNY and a former chef, he currently is Program Director at an educational facility for the elderly on Manhattan's Upper West Side.

Adrienne Rich has been active for fifteen years in the lesbian/feminist movement. Her most recent collection of poems is *Your Native Land, Your Life* (W. W. Norton, 1986), and her collection of essays, *Blood, Bread, and Poetry,* appeared in the same year. Her new volume of poems is *Time's Power.* She lives in California with the novelist Michelle Cliff and is an active member of New Jewish Agenda.

Mark Rudman's *By Contraries: Poems 1970–84* appeared in 198⁻ has also published a book of criticism, *Robert Lowell: An Introduction to the Poetry.* He has received fellowships from the Ingram Merrill Foundation and the New York Foundation of the Arts and is Assistant Director of the Graduate Writing Program at New York University, where he edits the literary journal *Pequod.*

Stephen Sandy is the author of four previous collections: *Stresses in the Peaceable Kingdom, Roofs, Riding to Greylock,* and, most recently, *Man in the Open Air.* He has been the recipient of numerous grants and awards for his poetry, the Academy of American Poets Prize and an Ingram Merrill Award among them. He teaches at Bennington College and lives in North Bennington with his wife and two children.

Ron Schreiber is a professor of English at the University of Massachusetts at Boston. His collections of poetry include *Tomorrow Will Really Be Sunday.* The poems "still alive" and "your life" are from his book *John* (co-published by Hanging Loose and Gay Presses of New York).

Maureen Seaton's poems have appeared in *The Iowa Review, Outlook, New Letters, The Mississippi Review,* and many other journals. She lives in New York City.

Charlie Smith's books include two works of fiction, *Canaan* (Avon Books) and *Shine Hawk* (Paris Review Editions), as well as a book of poems, *Red Roads,* which Stanley Kunitz chose for the 1987 National Poetry Series. Mr. Smith lives in New York City.

William Jay Smith is the author of more than a dozen books of poetry, including *Celebration at Dark, New and Selected Poems,* and *Laughing Time.* In 1970, he served as Consultant in Poetry to the Library of Congress. He lives in New York City.

Laurel Speer's latest book of poetry is *Very Frightened Men.* She also writes a monthly column of literary opinion for *Small Press Review* and a bimonthly book review sheet for *Book Call,* New Canaan, Connecticut.

Elizabeth Sullam was born and educated in Italy. Her book of poems, *Out of Bounds,* was published by Scripta Humanistica, Potomac, Maryland.

David Trinidad was born and raised in Southern California. His books of poetry include *Monday, Monday* (Cold Calm Press, 1985), *November* (Hanuman Books, 1987), and *Pavane* (Illuminati, 1988). He currently lives in Brooklyn, New York, where he teaches at Brooklyn College.

Jean Valentine was born in Chicago, graduated from Radcliffe College, and has written five books of poetry, most recently *Home. Deep. Blue: New and Selected Poems.* She lives in New York City and teaches at Sarah Lawrence College and the West Side Y for the Writer's Voice.

Chester Weinerman has been pursuing the double career of general law practice and writing for fifteen years. His poetry has been published in *The American Poetry Review, Partisan Review, Christopher Street,* and *New York Quarterly.* He lives in Brookline and Provincetown, Massachusetts.

Miller Williams teaches at the University of Arkansas, where he is the editor of the University of Arkansas Press. His books of poetry include *A Circle of Stone, So Long at the Fair, The Only World There Is,* and *Halfway From Hoxie: New and Selected Poems.*

Copyright
Acknowledgments